Believe in Yourself

Believe In

Yourself

Business Essentials for the
Millennial Entrepreneur

Jaebadiah S. Gardner

GardnerGlobal, Inc.

For information about book readings, speaking engagements, guest appearances
or podcast interviews, email: contact@gardnerglobal.com or call 206.623.1844

For information about permission to reproduce selections from this book, write to:
GG Publishing, LLC at contact@gardnerglobal.com

For information about special discounts for bulk purchases, please contact
GG Publishing, LLC at: contact@gardnerglobal.com or 206.623.1844

Gardner, Jaebadiah S.
Believe In Yourself (#BIY): Business Essentials for the Millennial Entrepreneur

Jaebadiah S. Gardner

Twitter @Jaebadiah
Instagram: Jaebadiah
Facebook: Jaebadiah Gardner

GardnerGlobal Publishing, LLC
1409 Post Alley
Seattle, WA, USA 98101

www.GardnerGlobal.com

Black.

Lives.

Matter.

Contents

CHAPTER 1

Passion

CHAPTER 2

Structure

CHAPTER 3

Relationships

CHAPTER 4

Haters

Preface

FAILED EARLY, FAILED FAST, AND FAILED OFTEN; THIS is the foundation of my empire. My attention span has always been short, especially with those who've bragged about all of their so-called wins but never been in a real fight, never had any real scars. I distance myself from those caught up on their own juice, and instead I have kept close those who practice humility. I have kept my eye on Father Time (or Mother Time or They Time) and the character it reveals in me & others. All I could ever really do is lead by example. I'm not claiming to be an expert in anything, but I am an expert of my own experiences.

Foreword

I WROTE THIS ON MY PHONE ON THE BUS. I WROTE THIS standing in a beer garden at Seattle's Folklife festival. I wrote this on several planes. I wrote this at home. I wrote this at my office. I wrote this in five countries. I wrote this at my other home—my parents'. I just wrote.

Now,

Venice, Italy is known by several names, one of which is the "Floating City." This is due to the fact that the city of Venice consists of 118 small islands connected by countless canals and bridges. Yet the buildings in Venice were not built directly on the islands. Rather, they were built upon wooden platforms supported by wooden stakes driven into the ground. A fair question arises: How could the Venetians use vertical wood pilings in the salt water for a foundation system without the wood rotting? The answer is counterintuitive. The wood is not exposed to oxygen as it is submerged in the water and mud, and as a result it does not rot. In fact, the wood becomes petrified due to a constant flow of mineral-rich water around and through it. In turn, the wood becomes a hardened, stone-like structure.

In a similar way, GardnerGlobal, Inc. was born out of a recession and experienced what it meant to build a lasting company that focuses on investment, partnerships and community. With longevity as our focus, we plan on opening the door for opportunities to experience real estate investment at its highest level. We started out undercapitalized, unsuspecting, and like the wood pilings that continue to hold up the city of Venice, we defied logic. And over time we've become stronger, leveraging contretemps and accepting of our natural elements to maintain strength. Far from weakening our foundation, the many challenges and adversity we have faced have only petrified our commitment to building wealth.

Where did #BIY (Believe in Yourself) come from? My step mother, Tamara Gardner made this collage when I was a freshman in high school when I had first moved up to Seattle. It was littered with positive quotes—dead center was the mantra, "Believe In Yourself." Years passed! I then graduate from college, I get my first job, I lose my first job, I start GardnerGlobal, Inc., I graduate from law school, and I begin to tweet #BIY with every post—"Believe in Yourself" over and over.

I began to wake up every morning telling myself, "Believe In Yourself." Then, one day Tamara tells me she's had this collage at home for years and that I should pick it up. I go home, pick it up, think nothing of it other than the great memories I had. Then it hits me, dead center of the collage: "Believe In Yourself.." And all this time, I thought I was the one who came up with the mantra . . .

She planted that #BIY seed in 1997 and I have sub-consciously been rolling with it ever since. With that said . . . words are powerful. May they lead you in the direction of your dreams.

Passion

"You reach a moment in life
when, among the people
you have known, the dead
outnumber the living."

—ITALO CALVINO

I. Monetize Your Passion

I DON'T THINK OF PASSION AS WHAT MOTIVATES OR
drives me. I tend to think of passion differently. Passion
to me is an obsession, a crazed state of mind that I enter
never to return. Passion is so deep that sacrificing becomes
a tranquil and mindless exercise. My passion is my para-
dise lost. Something a fleeting viral video can't come close
to entertaining. Most people make the mistake of acting off
impulse when inspired to work for themselves and starting a
business. One thing you must understand is that there are no
rules to this game of entrepreneurship—the only rules that
exist are the ones that you create for yourself. Starting a business is one thing, but maintaining your business is a whole
other pot-hole that one must know how to fill. Otherwise,
the road is going to be bumpy and you'll go flat, stagnant,
and eventually you'll end up hitch-hiking.

Now, don't get me wrong, I've met many people who have

taken the entrepreneur leap and instantly skyrocketed to financial and business success. For the most part, those folks are one out of every twenty people I come across. Nothing is impossible, but don't size yourself up to the next person. Everyone has his/her/their individual path. Speaking of individual paths, let's talk about your passion. [Crosses legs while sitting in the "GET OUT" therapist chair.] What is your passion? Have you found it? How long have you had it? The bigger question remains, can you monetize it? Are you ready to monetize it? How will you monetize it? I'll attempt to explore the latter questions and explain why I think it's an important place to start before you take that entrepreneurial leap.

Maybe you just got done watching a Tony Robbins speech, maybe you have a friend who's killin' the game and is a multimillionaire, maybe you just left a lecture at WeWork or Impact Hub and you're super motivated to start your own business—nothing can stop you, your fingers are moving on their own, your business plan went from one to ten pages overnight. You're chillin' with friends, spewing with energy and excitement about your new business. Family dinners are filled with you talking to mom and dad about how you're going back and forth about which company name to choose. Fast forward twelve months: You've changed jobs, made a slight pay increase, making enough scratch to take a couple trips, break off some bread to your family, and eat out at a couple happy hours. All the while, your dream is tucked away in a file on your Macbook Pro. Drinks with friends now include unspoken curiosities. While you're sitting across from them sipping on the courage juice, they are sitting across from you listening to you complain about your boss or talk about how your co-worker has B.O. All the while, they are thinking, what happened to that business you were supposedly starting that was going to completely change the world? My question to you is: Where did your passion go?

Like the settling of the Earth's soil, you slowly began to nestle into your comfortable space; you've seen this space before and know it all too well. Routine becomes your fixed income and sparks of motivation come alive when watching viral inspirational videos shared from a friend's timeline. (Although I may come off sounding condescending to this lifestyle choice, I'm not. You've heard the phrase, "to each their own." It's just an unfamiliar choice for me and when I express it, it sounds just like that, unfamiliar). Now, this is not to say that one choice is "better" than the other; it's just different, very different, and should be equally respected. The struggle, grit, and grind of an entrepreneur is not unlike that of someone who faces challenges within their corporate or hourly job and decides to professionally deal with situations in order to climb the ladder of corporate success. The co-worker competition, the insensitive things a boss might say, the constant beatdown of conformity. There is a lot of shit that gets crammed down people's throat, and to be able to swallow it in a graceful, professional and articulate way and still end up getting what you want is a true skill and damn near an art. For someone to climb the corporate ladder having gone through that gauntlet is something that should be celebrated because it is no easy task. And the reason why I can say this is because I used to work in that corporate environment. On top of the normal crap you get working a 9-to-5 job, I was an English major who had been hired by a general contractor, and for the life of people they couldn't figure out how I got hired. The racism and bias from that experience is enough to fill a whole other book. Maybe if my past co-workers are lucky, I'll write about that experience in my second book.

Now that I reserved my judgment for the 9-to-5 folks, let's get back to PASSION. I've never watched or listened to a Tony Robbins video. Not that I don't like the guy, it's just my passion operates on its own. It doesn't require the need to get temporarily motivated. My hunger is deeper than a

60-minute self-help lecture. When you're obsessed with what you do, you begin to speak another language. Words become superfluous and actions become the food that feeds your craze, and most importantly you become the living among the dead. Before starting your venture, it is critical to identify your passion clearly and articulately. Take some time on this. No need to rush into starting a business. Take a trip, have a scheduled walk, or sit and "think," what a concept! (Thinking is such an underrated exercise, more people should try it) Let it come to you, let the passion hit you like a monsoon that drowns out all haters, dissenters, and doubters. It should engulf you, consume you, and blind you to what you used to think was impossible. Wait for this feeling, and don't rush it. The universe will let you know when you're ready. And if you're someone who's lucky enough to have found your passion, you're one step ahead of the game.

Now here comes the tricky part. How do you convert that passion into dollars and cents? How do you take what you are obsessed with, what makes you the living among the dead, into a product or service that consumers will utilize? First, let's check in on your mindset, or your global paradigm, let's say. Are you a pessimist? Are you an optimist? Are you a realist? You should be a little bit of each. But if you were to have one more than the other, make sure your optimist tank is full. You're going to need every bit of it for this journey. Your realist tank? Well, that's what friends and family are for, to keep you grounded. You're pessimist tank? That's easy, that's what the "real world" is for, to chip away at your morale; you'll have enough people telling you, you can't do it. It is critical that you maintain a level of optimism that does not waiver, this is what will assist you in monetizing your passion. Now, I admit, this may be sounding a bit theoretical but entertain me for a second. If you are someone who considers themselves creative, then monetizing your passion may not be such an issue for you. But I'm not talking about artsy creative. I'm talking about business creativity. You'll need both a heightened sense of optimism and business creativity. I am a firm believer (optimist) that you can monetize just about anything! If you've traveled the world and hit third world or developing countries, you should notice that the depravity in the economic climate has forced a large majority of people to be entrepreneurs.

For example, in Mexico City I stopped by a street vendor who had large and small bottles, what looked like old 22oz and 40oz bottles of alcohol. He had beautiful paintings on each of them, all different. While asking him about his artwork, he began to tell us that he would dig for the bottles in recycle bins or trash cans, clean them thoroughly, and then paint and sell them. Every day, he took a completely priceless and used item and turned it into a fuckin' business. I didn't ask if that's what he was passionate about, but given the circumstances in Mexico City, you have to be selling something if you want to feed yourself and your family. The hustle is real (We'll get to this concept later). For this person in Mexico City, the driver could have been a few different things, but if you told someone you were going to dig through trash cans for bottles, clean, paint, and sell them, you will have a fair amount of people pat you on the back and wish you the best. You'll need to maintain your optimism and believe that anything you create you can sell.

II. What's the Plan? Build it out

Selling your idea or passion is not going to happen immediately either. Your level of patience is critical to the viability of your business. You'll need to play with several models. Revert back to your mindset: If you continually keep the words, can't, probably, almost, I don't know, maybe, I think so, within your vocabulary, I'll tell you right now, you're creating unnecessary mental hurdles for yourself. As I mentioned previously spending time with finding your passion, equally, you're going to absolutely need to spend time playing with different business models that will allow you to monetize your passion. Several models exist:

1. The direct sales model (e.g., Avon Herbalife)
2. The freemium model (e.g., Spotify)
3. The franchise model (e.g., McDonald's)
4. The Subscription model (e.g., Netflix)

Your homework: research each.

Do not limit yourself to these models. In fact, there are several more. I wanted to give you a flavor of types to get you thinking about your structure. Part of your planning process should be centered around how you create avenues for your future clients to access your product or services. You may be asking, how do I know which model is for me? Don't be afraid to test out different models, that is part of this exercise. Sometimes, you're able to include several models in one business. For example, take Nordstrom's, a direct sales and subscription company and they have bobbed and weaved into an online power-house. For now, just focus on one way to create revenue. Once you've settled on which model you think will serve you best, write it down. (Don't take on too much) The next step is to plan it out. Is this a monthly, daily, hourly income-producing model? Whichever it is, you'll need to map out the first 5 years. Seem daunting? Take it one year at a time and build out your projections of income against your expenses. Do this year by year. I can't stress enough how important it is for you to write down your model. You should be able to create a visual of how your business model works. I liken starting a business to someone who irregularly goes to the gym (I have all kinds of business analogies, deal with it). If you walk in on random days of motivation, you most likely lack a plan of what you're going to work out, and if you do, you'll see little to no progress with your physical features because you're not doing it regularly. In order to see dramatic changes with your body, you need to be consistent. Same with your new business. Consistency with your optimism and consistency with your business creativity. You need to spend time working brain muscles that you're not used to working. This is why it takes time to get in the right mindset. You need to train your mind every single day. Spending time in your obsession will force you to find the right model that works for you. In short, you need this plan. Write it out and watch destiny manifest itself. You can have all the passion in the world but if you don't make the time to hone it in an organized fashion, then you're wasting your time.

III. Sticking to the Vision at All Cost

It's easy to get distracted. Especially these days! Most millennials did not grow up with social media, but we became the earliest adopters. We've been socialized to believe instant gratification is an actual fact of life when really, it's an alternative fact. Our attention span runs faster than Usain Bolt, and we may frequently leave work and ideas unfinished. I bet all the unfinished business ideas from our generation could fill every landfill in the world. I would bet double or nothing that you already have a fair amount of those ideas in those landfills. So, how do you prevent your idea, dream, passion from ending up in a landfill?

Stick to your vision at all cost! What this means is eliminating all distractions. And I'm not joking, all distractions. Whatever your vices, you need to start building a commitment within yourself to quit that shit. That's not to say you can't indulge. What I'm saying is you should be indulging in your obsession. There's going to be time for everything else. With the exception of family, for me, everything else is by the wayside. You must remain focused on the task at hand and right now, it's getting everyone to believe that paying for your product or services is more than just supporting your dream—you will add value to their lives as well. But you can't do this if you get derailed from your track.

I see it all the time. People start a business. Step 1. Con-gratu-fuckinglations. They never make it to Step 2—Maintaining the business—because they got side-tracked by the next shiny and bling-y opportunity. Instead of going straight, they either veered left or right for one of two reasons: life happened and personal obligations kicked in, e.g. had a kid, got married, a family member passed, they were pressured by their spouse to get a "real job," or they did not have the patience to wait for their business to begin generating sufficient revenue, so they jumped ship.

If you have a vision, a painted picture in your mind of what your future looks like, you must hang it up front and center of your mind's wall so you wake up every morning and go to bed every day with that vision. Here are a couple things I do that help me maintain my vision:

I wake up every single morning and I tell myself one phrase. I repeat this phrase over and over under my breath as I look into my closet for what to wear. I say it in my mind over and over as I brush my teeth. I say it over and over when I'm in the shower. I'm saying this phrase over and over until I walk out the door. And when I have days when I wake up and forget to remind myself to say this phrase, I get pissed off at myself and I begin to repeat it in my mind. Sometimes I'll be in a meeting, sometimes I'll be getting coffee. It doesn't matter where I am when I remember—I am sure to keep routine. Would you like to know what phrase I tell myself every morning? Maybe the next book.

The second thing I did was I wrote a check to myself. I wrote it for an amount I will not disclose here, but I wrote it. "Put it down on paper." I just choose to use a check. In the memo line where it says "for," I wrote "persistence, hard work and dedication."

I'm sharing with you what I did/do to maintain my vision, but If you write it on your bathroom mirror or leave written notes to yourself in weird places of your house, that's fine. The key is you need reminders. Do whatever works for you.

Ah, yes, one of my favorite sub-topics. What's so interesting about this topic for me, at least, was I started out the business giving away so much free time to projects. I was helping organizations build websites, I was event planning, shit, at the early stages of the company, I was doing everything but real estate. That volunteer work turned into short-term contracts and eventually turned into what's now today a force of a real estate company. Why was I building websites for others and event planning? These were things I was doing to keep my business alive. I built the first couple revisions of the GardnerGlobal, Inc. website through Wordpress, so I came back to Seattle to hustle that skill. Let's be clear, every skill I gained starting my business, I hustled it out for "paper" (money to the layperson). But first it was free work.

Early on, I knew that Seattle was a finicky city and operated off of relationships. So this essential may or may not relate based on your location but either case I'm going to fill you in—when it comes to time. (Side note: You should also be thinking of your business in regards to your location/city. Demand/supply, study your city. Study the people. Find out how hard it's going to be to crack early on before you jump all the way in.) You may be required to do some free work up front when starting your business. Why? Unless you started your business with a Rolodex of ready-to-go clients, it's going to take some time for people to trust that you know what you're doing and quite honestly it's going to take time for you to trust yourself with what you're doing.

If you're Black you'll understand this metaphor, but your business at this stage of offering a product or service is like growing out your hair and being stuck in the middle stage. You have no fucking idea what to do with it. Too long to brush, too short to braid, curl, or twist. It's awkward to say the least. As a new business owner you may feel this awkwardness. You have a product/service but you have no idea how to deploy and get people to make use of it. So . . . you'll have to put in some free time or ship out some free products. (Yes, in your startup budget, account for everything going out and nothing coming in.)

Do not be afraid to put up free work. This is crucial to getting your name out and in all realness, that's the start of your branding. Here's a suggestion, offer your services to non-profits and community groups to start. Why, you ask? Great question! What I have found is non-profits are always in need of something, as well as community groups. Identify the need or investigate the need desired and fill it! Let them know that you'll do this first project pro bono. You may have to do a couple of these projects for a couple different groups, and that's okay. Like I said, unless you're an attorney, accountant or other professional who's worked in an industry for several years and you decide to jump ship and take ready-to-go clients, the struggle is about to be real. Free work has a bad wrap. You know how much shit I've learned doing free work? It was my testing grounds for my services. It allowed me the time to make mistakes, build relationships, and learn some crucial real-life business lessons you can't learn in school. You'll be forced to make decisions that may or may not work out to your advantage, and that's okay. You're period of free work is a stage to experiment and achieve professional growth. Some say that if it's free you're not going to get the best type of service or product. I took the mindset that no matter how much I got paid or didn't get paid, free or not, my name was attached to that work and I was always going to put my best effort forward. Why?? Reputation! Use this time of free work to build your reputation. That's the secret ingredient you're looking for at this point. But, I repeat, do not half-ass on the free work. Once you've established that you can knock the project out of the park guess what's going to happen when you're done? Yup, you got it. You're getting a call from your new client asking for more of that goodness. At this point, you can negotiate a fair fee for your services.

Don't get greedy and hit them over the head with a heavy fee or price for the product; ask them what they would be willing to pay.

Once you've crossed this bridge, you are now actually in business. Proceed with caution with free work. I made the mistake of jumping into giving so much of it that I wasn't getting paid anything. But I was giving so much time to my community. If you don't pay attention, the community will suck you dry. Suck you dry of time, your intellectual capacity and your family life. Even before I had anything they were asking for everything. I don't blame them for that. They were just trying to fill a void but this is what separates business-minded people from community-minded people.

You cannot be scared to say no to doing free work. How do I know when I should stop doing free work? At this point, if no one is calling you back asking you for more of that goodness you "thought" you served up then you need to keep working on your craft. You need to get your service or product to the point where you can negotiate a fee/price. If that isn't happening then keep working. Do not expect this to happen after your first project, it may take several.

Remember, you're using this time to hone your craft, build relationships, and build your reputation. The trick becomes, when do you stop the free work? This isn't easy to answer and will vary per circumstance. If the client you're working for is not coming to you with a dollar in hand for your service/product, then you need to be the one that starts the conversation because what it ultimately boils down to is, what is the value of your time?

What are you worth? Are you worth $200/hr? Are you worth $5.90/hr or somewhere in between? How do you value yourself? How does the client value you? You need to seriously ask yourself these questions. If you get stuck in the labyrinth of free work, your time is always going to be worth $0.00. And that's not a sustainable business model. I had made the mistake of giving so much so soon that everyone just expected me to keep working for them for free. At that time, I was doing anything and everything to make a buck. Yeah, I hoe'd myself out, but I needed to start somewhere. My free labor and penny-pinched labor involved but was not limited to: building websites, acting as a moving company, charging others to start businesses, and social media training. I did all kinds of shit. I just hustled—After a while of performing free work and having that discussion with those early clients, some let me go and wanted nothing to do with me. Some wished me luck. The only thing that mattered was whatever I did for them for that moment of freeness, they could never say I did crap work. Do some work for free, build your credibility, and then value your time.

Structure

"What we do is more
important than what we say
or what we say we believe."

—BELL HOOKS

I. What's your business model?

WHEN YOU HAVE TAKEN THE TIME TO IDENTIFY
and monetize your passion, you must begin to
think about what type of business model will best
fit your goals. I mentioned a few different types of business
models in Chapter 1, and I'm assuming you have already
thought about how long you want to be in business—Five
years? Ten years? Perpetually?

Knowing your business life timeline will help you decide
what type of business model to pursue. For my type of business and model, I knew there was an extremely long lead time
on when revenue would be generated. In addition to the odds
of a general business not generating revenue within the first
3 to 5 years of operation, I knew that becoming a real estate
developer would take even longer. For perspective, when Jeff
Bezos started Amazon, it took the company 7 years before
he went from red to black.

And unlike some entrepreneurs, I didn't come from
resources or have a trust fund to tap to start my business.

Not only that, I didn't have the resources to begin investing in and developing real estate; I had to somehow create those resources. And if you know real estate development you know that projects don't come easy and you don't get paid anything up front. So I started a "vertically integrated" business.

In microeconomics and management, vertical integration is an arrangement in which a company owns its own supply chain. Usually each member of the supply chain produces a different product or (market-specific) service, and the products combine to satisfy a common need. The business of real estate is wide and deep, which means there are a plethora of ways to maximize revenue. In other words, instead of creating a business that allowed for only one source of revenue, I situated my business to take in multiple sources of income all while serving the mission and vision of the company.

At GardnerGlobal Inc., our three specialty service lines are development, management, and brokerage. Our supply chain revolves around services—I wanted to ensure we were at all the service stops possible that generated revenue. I mention revenue a lot, but in fact that's not the most important takeaway from having a vertically integrated business. What's important is that you have complete ownership and control over those services or products you offer. In short, you control the branding, the team, and the direction. If not, then you're relying on a third party or "middle-man" to come through with that part of the product or service. So that's money out, not money in. It didn't make sense to me to contract out those services to someone else when we could keep it in house.

Most real estate companies are exclusively brokerages, which means they only buy and sell. Other real estate companies are exclusively property management companies, while others do both. Not often do you come across a company that does all three. I had watched my mentors for years, and before I even studied real estate I had studied their business model. I learned about their structure and how they were

organized, and then I started focusing on learning the real
estate business. I started off as a property management company and my partner, Damon McGruder, who had a managing broker's license, was able to offer the brokerage service to the company. By having both of those services in-house, we were able to refer both brokerage deals internally and property management opportunities internally. Some people are buying their second or third home or moving out of state, it's been nice to be able to make the commission and then make the residual monthly management fee. Whereas commission is a one-time deal, property management is residual.

Decide on a business model that's going to get you through lean times and test it. If that model doesn't work, you know what's so crazy? You have the ability to test a new one! What? How crazy is that? Don't give up if your first model is not as fruitful or as smooth as you would like it. Think about the first time you tried to ride a bike—what happened? Odds are you most likely fell on your ass at least a few times before you were able to ride it by yourself. The reason why you got better and didn't need any help is because you practiced enough to figure out how to balance. It's the same with your business model—unless you've done it before, be prepared to fall on your ass. Get back up and keep trying. If that model doesn't work, like riding a bike, switch up your technique. Often, the tiniest adjustment makes all the difference.

II. Organization is key

I built my business model around longevity which meant that I could not just rely on one source of income. With development being highly complicated, I needed other avenues that would allow me to bring in cheese. As I mentioned previously, I had no idea all the different pockets for potential revenue; line items I could incorporate in my Profit and Loss sheet. But once I learned it, it was "game-on"! Hustle and motivate! What does your business model look like? Have you spent time with your mentors asking them questions about how they organized their business? From a very basic level you need to understand what type of business entity they chose. S-Corp? C-Corp? LLC? Non-profit? Special Purpose Corporation? Do you have a basic understanding of what separates each? I'm not going to get into the differences of each entity, that's your homework. But I will tell you that having a basic understanding of business organization will be extremely helpful. If you do not have a mentor who's a business owner you can either (1) identify one, or (2) pull up some of your favorite local brands or similar types of businesses and begin to study them. We live in the information era, so there's damn near nothing you can't find. Find out how they are structured and most importantly, why they chose that structure. Everything will eventually come down to how well you're organized. Whether seeking investors or new hires, you'll need to have some type of system in place. If you create the space for what you need, then you'll begin to see the desired people and resources fall into that space. Some have a stroke of luck—the first venture they create brings in over and beyond what they were expecting. The vast majority of entrepreneurs will take a number of shots creating until they find that frequency that touches their audience. Then that space gets filled exactly how they planned it.

Here's what I've witnessed: I see my fellow entrepreneurs and business owners fall into a couple traps. First, they have so many ideas that they can't settle on one, or they have so many ideas they can't seem to finish the first idea before moving onto the next. So they end up with tons of unfinished ideas. Second, they simply have no structure and organization around their first idea. They have an idea that works, they have a demand that can be met with their product of service, but they have no way to accept online payments, they have no invoice system, a team that can execute without them being present or any means to make closing the deal an efficient and smooth process for the client. In addition, they keep running that same tired old system into the ground, refusing to try something new. Man, I feel this so much as I write it. I had to beat my head against a brick wall for at least 5 years until I woke up to make those changes necessary to grow. And you should know I'm still making adjustments, trying to fine tune what makes folks want to engage us on a business level. Times change, technology changes. Sheeeitt! People change. You should be ready to change as well. Some businesses that couldn't make that change and had to file for Chapter 11 bankruptcy in recent years. Remember Block-buster Video? Or Toys R Us?

Although I named two large corporations, that fact should be even more thought-provoking. Some of these companies have been around for 20+ years and they went out of business. One would assume that because these companies have been in business so long, the executive leadership have figured it all out. And I'm not saying that the above-mentioned busi-nesses that filed Ch. 11 couldn't necessarily adapt to change. Each company had their own demons to fight internally, but I would make the assertion that the aforementioned brick-and-mortar companies were not as open to change and as they should have been. Be willing to organize and reorganize.

This leads me into the next subtopic of "personnel." How you organize your team and the people you hire will cre-ate and perpetuate the company culture you set forth. As a millennial in a widely Baby Boomer and silent generation industry, I wanted to ensure that my team was not just filled with folks from my generation; I wanted as much age diver-sity as possible, leaning to the side of having more Gen Y and Millennial perspectives. My partner is part of the Boomer generation and my interns are from the Gen Z generation, then you have us Millennials in the middle. This age diversity does several things: (1) The younger people we bring on board always bring a new perspective to the table. This point of view may be new to us but it is very common for them. They give us the most boots-on-the-ground information in terms of social media, new tech being used, but most importantly a consensus of how their age group is thinking, particularly around real estate. We leverage that information to tailor our marketing and public relations. And (2) the older more seasoned people on the team add invaluable historical and experience context around us bright-eyed and bushy-tailed young conquerors. The GardnerGlobal board is made up of three millennials and three baby boomers.

Be hyper-strategic with who you bring onboard your team. Make sure their values align with the company values. They are many reasons why someone will want to work with and for you; it's up to you to decipher if those reasons vibe with your vision. Remember that actions speak louder than words and know that a resume or interview does not in any way tell you what kind of person you're interviewing. I honestly could care less about someone's resume. I want to hear from their mouths what they've done, what their excited about and what they plan on contributing. If they have issues verbalizing those three things then I know they're faking the funk. Some are great at the "fake it 'til you make it" move and that's fine but at a certain point, they'll expose themselves. The question for you is as a future employer, do you have the time and money to find out? I can't lie, the people-part of the business is the toughest part; at least for me it has always been challenging. While there is much you can control, people are ultimately "crap shoots." You just never know. The only thing that's been helpful for me on the personnel front is time and experience. I've dealt with tons of people in the past 10 years and have honed a radar that detects all the bullshit. And more importantly, I have a clearer image of the type of person I want on the team. It's hard to find what you're looking for in the early part of the business because you've been through limited struggles. You will reach a point when, after dealing with so many personality types, certain ones will become uber apparent to you because you're experience has taught you

and your intuition will guide you. The only way to find out
is to put your money up and take the risk.

Do you hire staff before your start generating the revenue
to sustain your business, or do you wait to generate the sufficient amount of revenue to hire? Don't be too hard and fast
with deciding if certain "things" should happen. Have a plan
for sure. Again, we're talking structure. Here's what I would
recommend: Draw boxes with titles underneath them, not
just titles but titles of roles you need to fill. Example: "Executive assistant." Fill out as many boxes as you think you need.
Under the titles, write down the daily tasks that person with
that title will be doing. Do this according to your company
needs. Do you need someone to do marketing? If so, what
does that mean in regards to tasks? Do you need someone
to be the bookkeeper? What is your bookkeeper going to be
doing? Be specific with those tasks. If you don't know what
that role entails, make no excuses. Ask Google.

Don't think about money, think about a scenario where
you could staff all the way up today. What would your company look like? After you have made the boxes and written
down the titles and tasks, start filling in names in those boxes.
They could be people you know, just met, or want to meet.
Put a star next to the box that you need the most. If you
can't think of a name, leave it empty. The names may change
and the boxes may change, too, but at least you have a visual
of who's going to be executing on certain tasks. You as the
entrepreneur cannot do it all. You will hit a wall and the
pressures will give rise to doubt. Realize when you have to
let go and trust. After all, if you hire someone and you can't
trust them to do the work, then think about what that is
really speaking to. Your new team member's success depends
on how well you trained them. Your ability to communicate
is important, but it's secondary. What is ever more important is understanding how your team members communicate.
Honestly, as I look back I wish I had a deeper understanding of basic communication and learned how each of my

team members communicated. Maybe they would still be on the team, maybe they would have added significant revenue value, maybe, just maybe.

For myself, I knew what I needed in regards to getting it all done on a daily. I also knew that I didn't want to hire robots. As a small business we have so much flexibility—I want people on the team to be able to build out their positions as long as it was within the parameters of the company values and mission. This means that I am seeking motivated individuals to work in GardnerGlobal, Inc. Yes, I would give direction and the team member had certain tasks, but I'm not a micro-manager. I would leave it up to the team member to build out their schedule and workload. I give them absolute freedom over their work, but at the exchange of superior execution and delivery. Remember, your team should be the reason your business thrives. Write it down, talk it out, and get organized.

Relationships

"Never burn bridges,
unless it's rickety,
then build your own "

—TAMARA GARDNER

I. Where do you Spend Your Time?

THE MOST VITAL AND PRECIOUS ITEM YOU HAVE IS time. You can't get it back. Do you think of time like a currency that you exchange? How much of it do you have and where do you spend it? Time is another critical essential you need to understand—this will separate you from the rest of your perceived competition. Most people have no idea what they want to do, so they either lollygag or they stew in purgatory not knowing where to go. Why am I being so abstract? A wise person once told me that time is relative. Everyone spends it differently. What seems to you like 5 years might only be 5 minutes for another person. Getting a feel for time—especially its complexity, and how you fit in that realm—will assist you greatly in your business endeavors.

Are you hitting networking events arbitrarily? Showing up to anything that says "young professionals" or "happy hour" will not be beneficial to you. If you're starting a business you need to get more focused than that. If you want to go just to lightweight mingle, get a drink, and exchange a couple cards, then I would say hit up one of those functions. But if you're trying to build a client base and establish relationships, you need to have more of a strategic and tactical approach. You should be spending time in places that are initially directly in line with your passion. Why? You'll meet like-minded individuals who share your passion and potentially vision. These people will become your collaborators and supporters.

If you think sending out one email, having one conversation, or showing up to one networking event or company party is going to get you to where you want to go . . . NEWS FLASH! IT WILL NOT! Like most things, being an entrepreneur is all about consistency. You need to consistently show your face at events that most pertain to your industry. This begs the question, in what membership groups are you involved in? If none, then you need to be thinking about what groups/organizations you can get involved with early. The reason why you need to do this ASAP is these organizations will be hosting events, creating other opportunities for businesses like yours to meet, network, offer informationals, and who knows what else. Depending on the group, the resources will vary. Do some homework on your industry's "typical" memberships groups. Right off the bat, you need to have clarity on two things: 1) Get an understanding of what it is your company needs; and 2) Research the orgs/groups you are looking to become a member of, and with accuracy, state the exact benefits your company will receive by becoming members. Line up your company needs with the benefits you will receive. Once you do this, research that group's events calendar and plan to show up at their events at least once a month. If you want to go further, involve yourself deeper. Ask about volunteer opportunities at the events they host. Maybe there are small committees that are planning events or other activities that you can serve on? As a new business, the purpose here is to build relationships and to build trust, which doesn't happen with one introduction email or attendance at one event. The more people see you, the more they trust you. They might not even know what it is your do or know what your company offers, but for some reason they'll feel comfortable exploring the idea of working with you or referring you out to someone else for business. Lastly, be regular—be as consistent as your bowel movements. Otherwise, you're wasting your time and we all know how valuable that can be . . .

Simultaneously, as you fill your calendar with strategic events to hit, make sure you have a mentor or mentors on your side. If you're going to be spending your time developing and executing your business plan, you need to make time to follow up with those who have been around the block a number of times. If you don't have anyone you can call/email and discuss the inner struggles that you face, then you need to identify some folks ASAP. Ideally, these mentors have proven themselves successful in the industry that you're looking to break into. You need an oracle, or ideally, a number of oracles. That's what I call my mentors: oracles.

Mentors have played a gigantic role in the growth of my real estate business. It's 2019 and I first met these mentors back in 2009. They are my friends and my compass. I looked into the real estate industry and tried to find the developers operating at the highest tier and set out to meet with them. These were other real estate developers and business owners. My title was "Founder & CEO" and I was not going to meet with anyone who didn't share that title. I needed to meet with folks who understood the full weight and gravity of their title and I wanted to know what they knew. Don't be afraid to reach out to someone you admire and ask to sit for a cup of coffee. All my mentor relationships involved me reaching out numerous times, following up numerous times, and calling numerous times. The art of the follow-up. I wanted to meet with these people and there was nothing that was going to stop me from doing so. If you are looking to meet with other C-level executives, don't be scared. "Scared money never made money." Yes, they are busy. Yes, they are also running companies. Yes, you may feel intimidated because they seemingly have so much more of everything than you. But don't let that get in your head. Keep following up. At some point they will reach back out to you and set up a first "date." If you've been at the follow-up for a couple months and hear crickets, then I suggest going down to their office and asking for them. I've done this with one of Seattle's largest developers. His name was Martin Selig. I called, emailed, called, emailed. . . I can't remember how many times. After about a couple months, I walked into his office downtown and asked for him. The receptionist told me he was busy or out, I don't recall. Either case, the next day, Seattle's billionaire real estate developer, Martin Selig called my cell phone.

Be persistent when working with your mentors. Keep them close. Make up reasons to meet with them. Remember, what you're looking to do is something they've done countless times. They have the answers. The funny thing is they won't share all the goods at the first few meetings—they don't know you, why should they?— but after they get to know you, keep your pen and pad ready because the advice they will give you will be worth more than any check they could write you. Find a mentor(s), follow up, and listen.

The great thing about having mentors is they will occasionally invite you to galas, receptions and events that you would most likely not have access to due to cost or lack of knowledge of the event. Exposing you to new environments and bringing you into their circle is their way of helping. TAKE IT!!! Use that space and work the room. Bring your cards, get your game face on, research who attends, look at what companies are sponsoring the event and find those people and get their cards. Remember, we are talking about your time. How will you use it? It's easy to attend the dinner, eat the food, and sit there like a bump on a log. But don't forget that opportunities are all around you.

These essentials can be difficult for introverts. I understand why. Even for extroverts, attending an event where you know only one person can be intimidating. If this is the case, take a moment to reflect on why you are going? Tap back into that passion that you're obsessed with. If walking up to a stranger and introducing yourself is too much for you, ask your mentor to introduce you to who you would like to meet. Have a list of people you want to meet ready to go. For instance, I'll hit events with 100-plus people in the room, and depending on the event and my goal, I'll show up to meet one person and one person only. After I've scanned the room, I'll make sure to get in front of that person and get what I need, either face time or a card. Whatever it is, I can leave having uttered the words, "mission accomplished." I don't mean this lightly—feel accomplished when you leave that event. Enjoy the bougie meal and ambience, but take advantage of the connections. That's why you're there. Don't get caught up in the superficial facade of the event. It's your time. I've shaken the hand of my idol, a billionaire real estate developer and President Barack Obama's good friend. This was based off a relationship who allowed me access to the room. I took it upon myself to seek and destroy—I wasn't going to leave without meeting my idol. And all the while, I consider this work. So should you.

Furthermore, if you do not have a mentor or someone who can clue you in on the events where you need to be, research and find these events yourself. Most often, there will be fundraisers or community events. There have been countless times where I had neither the connections nor the money to get into a fundraiser or event. I wouldn't let that stop me from getting in front of people. I would throw on my recycled suit—which I kept alive by strategically changing shirts and ties—and I would show up an hour into the event and walk in. Usually at this time the people checking for tickets or money are eating or running around and not at the entry table. I would walk past the entry table, and knowing from experience that not every seat will be occupied, I would walk into the ballroom or event and look for the obvious empty seats. This tactic was a great way for a starving start-up business owner to get a free meal and be in the room with influencers. In summary, get creative and don't let the lack of money or "people resource" hold you back.

II. Leverage

If you are not accustomed to using this word, start to incorporate it in your everyday language. Traditionally, "leverage" gets used in the context of loans, such as using capital to its maximum advantage. Here's a new definition for you: "Maximum advantage." Have you applied maximum advantage to your network? Everyone you know within your network has value, different value but value nonetheless. The question is do you know how to leverage your network? Have you ever attempted to use something to the maximum advantage? How did that work out for you? What was the end result? Was it beneficial? If you have not utilized something to the maximum advantage, why is that? Is fear holding you back? What are you fearful of? These are questions you should begin to explore. As a new or upcoming business owner, you'll need to master this essential. Unless you're Jeff Bezos, whose parents gave him $300,000 to start Amazon, you'll need to learn how to maximize every bit of resource at your disposal. At some point, even Jeff Bezos had to figure out how to get the "maximum advantage" out of his parents' money.

Before you begin to think about using something to its maximum advantage, though, you need to carefully identify your needs. Knowing what you need will help you be precise with utilization of your resources. This is extremely important because you don't want to be barking up the wrong tree. If your story is anything like mine and didn't have parents with $300,000 to give you a head start and a ton of human capital to utilize, then you need to get creative about what you leverage. This is when you're true hustler spirit will shine. I must confess, you can't teach hustle—either you've got it or you don't. Either you got it or you learned it. What does hustling have to do with leverage? A real hustler looks at most things as opportunities. Opportunities are what you leverage.

If you are a startup or thinking about starting a business, the most important item you can leverage is your human capital. Yes, money is important, but that's not going to get your little engine hot. There are two types of human capital buckets you must tap into. First, you'll need a strong internal support network; this is family, friends, mentors and "arm's length" supporters,or people you come across occasionally but regularly you don't really know too well, but who know you well enough to support your cause and vice versa. These peripheral supporters are a secret ingredient. The reason being is it's more important to have people saying positive things about you and your venture when you're not in the room. And in the case of your name coming up in circles where you're not there, you need these arm's length people corroborating on those positive statements. The second type of human capital that is extremely important is your team. At first you will need to do everything. You'll be the accountant, PR director, CEO, web builder, business developer, and much more. Notwithstanding this reality, you need to begin framing the people who you want to hire around the business. Having a strong team is ultimately crucial, vital, and necessary in order for your business to get off the ground and eventually thrive. You will need to leverage both groups of people to your "maximum advantage." Each person in your circle has something they can contribute to your mission. Forget about asking for checks—leverage your relationships. For example, if you need a website, tap into your local community college and four-year universities. Offer a three-month internship with a three-month timeline to complete your website. The student can get course credit and a portfolio-building experience and you get a free website.

Identify your company needs, where your skillset is lacking and ping your network to fill in those blanks. If it's not direct work, it could be more guidance you seek. Leverage your personal relationships to the hilt in order to connect with those people who've already done what you are setting out to accomplish. You'll find yourself three to four people deep from your initial contact person. This is good! This means your meeting people and hopefully learning something valuable from each connect. And remember, each connect has something to offer. Maybe sometimes they don't seem like it at first, at the very least, you had an opportunity to extend your vision and your mission. At the core of it all, shoot for longevity. I'll say it a second time: Stop seeking a check. Seek a relationship. Farmers don't harvest the day they plant seeds. It takes them seasons and sometimes the crops die. Depending on your business model, it has its own season. Have the long view. Stay patient and build on the relationships you have. Cultivate those. You'll have baskets to harvest and share at a later date.

III. Ask for Help

I must admit, this was (and sometimes still is) THE toughest essential to grasp and execute. Knowing myself, I am super prideful and a do-it-yourself-er. I hate asking for help. For such a long time, I viewed asking for help as a sign of weakness and that was the last thing I wanted to portray—a weak business owner and real estate developer. Plus, in my industry of real estate, there's no time for weakness. These waters are shark-infested and weak individuals will get eaten as soon as there's blood in the water. With that said, ask for help! ☺ There's no way you're going to get through this journey without help. You may like to think that you have everything under control and have the skillset to run a business, but unless you've done it before, you'll quickly hit a brick wall, burnout, exhaust your resources early, and you'll be back looking for a full-time job to work under someone else. So, remove your pride, know that you'll need help at every aspect of your business, and work smarter. It's about being efficient. When you are leveraging your resources, that is the time you ask for help. Here are some ways I phrase asking for help in conversations:

"If you were my age, what would you do when confronted with this situation?"
"What do you suggest I do Now?"
"What do you think I'm doing wrong?"
"Where can I improve?"
"What kind of resources would you ask for at this stage in business?"

It's important that you have your mentors and/or trusted confidantes get a sense of where you are at currently. Be honest. If you're broke, tell them. Not out of pity but because that's your real situation. What do you have to lose? You're already broke, right? In all seriousness, these mentors will be reminded of the exact moment in time when they were there, too, and this flashback will lead to invaluable advice. Put your pride aside and be vulnerable in a professional aspect. You have somewhere to go. Don't let pride get in the way of you getting there. Relationships will be the foundation of your business.

Haters

"If you have haters, that means you're doing something right"

—UNCLE BRUCE

I. Sucka MCs

Haters, A.K.A. Sucka MCs: Fuck 'em! I spent as much time on this chapter as I do with my haters. Take note.

It's Fucking Hard

"The world doesn't owe you shit"

—ANTHONY GARDNER

I. Pancakes

THERE'S STANDING FIRM, THEN THERE'S STANDING firm through the test of time. Perseverance might be the most essential tool in your kit. We all know the stats when it comes to startups—the desert of dry bones in *Lion King*. While they always share the number of businesses that fail, how much do you know about why those startup businesses did *not* survive? Did they run out of Capital? Have a bad marketing plan? Were there partnership issues? It doesn't make a difference. You need to do the homework and get a solid understanding of the reasons why those small businesses no longer exist. In particular, be smart about your research and look into failed businesses within your specific industry and maybe a few on the periphery of your industry.

Here are the top reasons why startups fail to go the distance (Michael Ames, Small Business Management):

1. Lack of experience
2. Insufficient capital (money)
3. Poor location
4. Poor inventory management

5. Over-investment in fixed assets
6. Poor credit arrangements
7. Personal use of business funds
8. Unexpected growth
9. Poor planning

Other reasons small businesses have a tough time making it, according to Moya Mason:

Choosing a business that isn't very profitable. Even though you generate lots of activity, the profits never materialize to the extent necessary to sustain an on-going company.

Inadequate cash reserves. Consider both business and personal living expenses when determining how much cash you will need. If you don't have enough cash to carry you through the first six months or so before the business starts making money, your prospects for success are not good.

Failure to clearly define and understand your market, your customers, and your customers' buying habits. Who are your customers? You should be able to clearly identify them in one or two sentences. How are you going to reach them? Is your product or service seasonal? What will you do in the off-season? How loyal are your potential customers to their current supplier? Do customers keep coming back or do they just purchase from you one time? Does it take a long time to close a sale or are your customers more driven by impulse buying?

Failure to price your product or service correctly. You must clearly define your pricing strategy. You can be the cheapest or you can be the best, but if you try to do both, you'll fail.

Failure to adequately anticipate cash flow. When you are just starting out, suppliers require quick payment for inven-

tory (sometimes even COD). If you sell your products on
credit, the time between making the sale and getting paid
can be months. If you fail to plan for it, this two-way tug at
your cash can pull you down.

**Failure to anticipate or react to competition, technology,
or other changes in the marketplace.** It is dangerous to
assume that what you have done in the past will always
work. Challenge the factors that led to your Success. Do you
still do things the same way despite new market demands
and changing times? What is your competition doing differently? What new technology is available? Be open to new
ideas. Experiment. Those who fail to do this end up becoming pawns to those who do.

Overgeneralization. Trying to do everything for everyone
is a sure road to ruin. Spreading yourself too thin dimin-
ishes quality. The market pays excellent rewards for excellent
results, average rewards for average results, and below average
rewards for below average results.

Overdependence on a single customer. At first, it looks
great. But then you realize you are at their mercy. Whenever
you have one customer so big that losing them would mean
closing up shop, watch out. Having a large base of small
customers is much preferred.

Uncontrolled growth. Slow and steady wins every time.
Dependable, predictable growth is vastly superior to spurts
and jumps in volume. It's hard to believe that too much business can destroy you, but the textbooks are full of case studies.
Going after all the business you can get drains your cash and
actually reduces overall profitability. You may incur significant up-front costs to finance large inventories to meet new
customer demand. Don't leverage yourself so far that if the
economy stumbles, you'll be unable to pay back your loans.

When you go after it all, you usually become less selective about customers and products, both of which drain profits from your company.

Believing you can do everything yourself. One of the biggest challenges for entrepreneurs is to let go. Let go of the attitude that you must have hands-on control of all aspects of your business. Let go of the belief that only you can make decisions. Concentrate on the most important problems or issues facing your company. Let others help you out. Give your people responsibility and authority.

Putting up with inadequate management. A common problem faced by Successful companies is growing beyond management resources or skills. As the company grows, you may surpass certain individuals' ability to manage and plan. If a change becomes necessary, don't lower your standards just to fill vacant positions or to accommodate someone within your organization. Decide on the skills necessary for the position and insist the individual has them.

Ultimately, this lack of self-criticism causes many companies—startups and their more mature counterparts alike—to fail. Startups suffer this fate more often because there are more dreamers than doers.

More often than not, businesses fail to get off the ground because of an insufficient supply of capital. Either the owner misjudged how much they would actually need to get things going (that and timing) or they didn't place the capital in the right location to grow.

With that said, don't get it twisted, it's not all about the capital. I started GardnerGlobal, Inc., with $4,500 in 2009 at the height of a recession. Not only that, but I wasn't starting a lemonade stand; the type of company I started was a real estate company. It's safe to say that I was more than under-capitalized. In short, I was drowning before I got started, and

I didn't even know I was drowning. Which is probably a good thing because I was fearless. And to be candid, I can't say today that I would have accepted this challenge if someone had laid out all of the crap that I would have to go through to be able to not only stand on my own twos but have the company stand on its own twos.

It's hard. It's fucking hard. You know why it's hard? It's hard because you won't have enough money to keep your company email active and it will shut down, and when clients and prospective clients email you, these messages will get bounced back to them and you'll look and feel like an idiot. It's hard because no one will believe in you or your mission. In actuality, other than your parents (*if* they are cool), few people will actually care about what you're doing. It's hard because you'll have family who will give up on you, disown you, purposely try and derail and break what you've built. It's hard because you won't have enough funds to pay people. It's hard because when you'll finally have enough to pay people, then those people will quit and you won't have anyone lined up to catch that workload. It's hard because you don't know what the fuck you're actually doing—that is, unless you've started, built and sold a company before. Ultimately, if you don't admit this to yourself, you're in for a serious blow to the ego.

Starting and maintaining a small business is like boxing. You'll get hit. And getting punched in the mouth is part of the game, but will you continually get hit in the same spot with the same punch? In other words, will you be able to recognize your mistakes, bounce back, and not repeat them? E-40 calls it "get back skills." Do you have "get back skills"? The ability to get knocked out but get back up to the place you were or even better your position? Perseverance is key, my friends.

What's difficult about maintaining your perseverance isn't the business wrinkles I just mentioned. On a deeper level, can you sustain the beatdown for a long period of time, all while maintaining your steadfast belief in yourself? Some would consider the beatdown as "taking losses," and others might instead treat them as learning lessons. There's a difference. Can you continually withstand being told "no"? Can you live on the fringes, barely making the rent/mortgage? How much struggle can you take before you throw in the towel and give up?

LOL! I'm laughing because as I write, I just remembered one particular Saturday morning during my second year of law school. I had woken up and decided to make pancakes for breakfast. After I put the large coil burner on 5, I dropped in some extra virgin olive oil, cracked an egg in a plastic bowl, and whipped up that batter with a dash of cinnamon. Mmm, I was ready for them 'cakes. I slowly poured the batter into the lopsided heated pan. You know what I'm talking about—the kind of pan that's so old it's unbalanced, leans on one side and cooks faster on the side that actually touches the coil! Anyway, I had made about two pancakes and the music was blasting in the back of my apartment when I heard a knock on the front door. I immediately turned the music down and walked to my door. At the time, I lived in an apartment building that had about 60 or 70 units. I opened the door and the person wearing a satchel was holding a mobile credit card reader.

"I'm looking for Jaebadiah," the man said matter-of-factly. Wearing my faded black tank top (because it had been washed about 700 times) and a pair of basketball shorts, I replied, "I'm Jaebadiah." "Well, Jaebadiah, you owe on your electricity bill and we need payment in full today in order to avoid service disruption." I told the man that I didn't have the money to pay but asked if he could give me a couple weeks to make a partial payment. He said, "Sorry, sir" and explained that he needed to take payment today or they would cut my electricity. Again, I repeated, "I don't have it." He said, "Ok," I said, "Ok," and I closed the door, walked back to turn up the music, and returned to the stove. I placed more batter in the

lopsided pan, bobbing my head to the music, buttering up the
two pancakes that were done, and all of a sudden, everything
went dark. Music stopped, all the lights and appliances went
out, and that was that. My third pancake didn't even get
flipped to the other side! I looked at my sad ass pancake and
thought, "Well, let's go ahead and cook this bad boy with the
heat that's left in the pan." I mean, I knew they were going to
cut my electricity but damn! Within minutes?! Wasn't ready
for that. I sat down eating my pancakes that Saturday morning in darkness and silence, but I laughed. Laughed with a
mouth full of pancakes. I'd take a bite and a sip of milk. I'd
do this repeatedly until my meal was done. I did this while
sitting at the table that I had dragged in from the back of
the apartment near the dumpster where someone had left it
as they moved out.

At that moment I looked around my empty apartment
and vowed, "Never again." Luckily I was scheduled to fly out
to Seattle a couple days later so I wouldn't have to spend my
days living in a third world country in my 1 bedroom Grand
Rapids, Michigan apartment.

At that time in my life, 2010, I was a law student paying
rent, school expenses, paying for business expenses, i.e. email
marketing, business email and paying (making up ½) of the
mortgage for my condo back in Seattle. I was living off of
financial aid which barely took care of my living expenses
in Grand Rapids and my legal studies. Additionally, I was
on unemployment from my job at Turner construction. I
would use my twice-a-month unemployment to pay off my
mortgage back in Seattle. During that time in the real estate
market, it was always a challenge to find a renter to cover
your mortgage. But hindsight is 20/20, and there are many
things I wished I would have calculated before I made that
investment. What most of this struggle did was make it really
difficult to focus on my legal studies. I knew at the end of
the day, I had to maintain my education as my top priority.
In addition, at Western Michigan Cooley Law School, if I

had more than three absences for any class in one semester, I would be dropped automatically from that class. Rain or shine, sick or healthy, they were not playing games. This is not a common practice among law schools. Most law schools, especially the "top tier" schools, don't take roll and could not care less if you showed up to class. If you passed the exam at the end of the semester, you moved on. Not WM Cooley Law School. They'll drop your ass in a heartbeat. What this meant is I couldn't slip and miss class because I simply felt like it. (Shout out to Western Michigan Cooley law school for teaching me a new level of self discipline) The pressures were real. And although the bank account was empty, the belief was strong and unwavering. Yeah, I got bent, but I didn't break. I kept myself showing up to class. I made sure my company email stayed active. I sacrificed for what I saw was longevity. The vision was to be around forever—at any costs, I would do whatever it took to keep GardnerGlobal, Inc., alive in this world.

To persevere is to never look back. Don't get me wrong, I'm not saying forget the past and forget what you've been through. I'm actually saying the opposite. You need to never forget what you've gone through. You must be fearless against the future problems to come, but commit to yourself that you'll never go back to hoping your pancake gets cooked by the leftover heat in the stove coil because your electricity just got cut off.

II. Survival

We didn't have any business but we were active and we were a real entity. You don't fail until you quit, stop, or cease, and you have to know that those three words are never an option. Not many people know how I survived through law school; when I first moved out to Grand Rapids, Michigan I had nothing. I literally slept on my clothes for padding because I didn't have a bed. I would eat hard-boiled eggs for dinner.

The Breakfast Group (a professional group of African American men) sent me a check for $3,500, which was enough to jumpstart my law school life in Grand Rapids. I bought a bed, went grocery shopping, bought books for my classes, and had rent covered for a couple months. Short-term survival for me was food stamps and collecting unemployment. I had been laid off from Turner Construction in January of 2009. I was collecting unemployment in March or so of 2009 all the way up to Year 2 of law school. Unemployment plus food stamps kept me just above water. There was a very special lady in my life at the time . . . she flew out to hang out with me for my birthday and for a birthday present she took me grocery shopping. We took the bus there and we took the bus back. Both with bags full of groceries. I remember walking through the frozen food section saying, "Happy birthday to me!" When she would leave back to Seattle, I would continue grocery shopping except I would shop at the gas station a block away. My head was down ten to twelve hours a day and there was no way I was up for a 30-minute bus ride to the nearest grocery store. So . . . what were my options? The local gas station. They had the basics. Milk, cereal, canned chili beans, and ass wipe.

My daily routine consisted of texting my best friends back home—Atuanya Priester and Morgan LaVance Powell—how depressed I was and how I just wanted to give up. I was alone, on an island, supposed to be there for school but also to grow this business I had started nine months prior. I didn't know how long I could hang on. There is only so much canned chili beans one can consume before they lose it! It wasn't all bad—I was very fortunate to have an extended Persian family in Seattle that made sure at the very least I had food. On my holiday trips back to Seattle, I would be greeted with pounds and pounds of frozen Persian food. Everything from cotlet, to khoresht Lubia and my favorite khormeh-sabzi. At that time, I had had a falling out with my immediate family and I had no support coming from that direction. My girlfriend at the time, and her mom and family stepped in to be a support network. I would come home to Seattle and against old school Persian tradition, the mom would let me stay at their house. How thankful was I? Barely holding on to what I had in Grand Rapids, Michigan to come home to a roof and food. It was the sweetest thing. She would freeze the food she had made a few days prior and have it ready for me to take with me on my flight back to Grand Rapids. Yes, I flew halfway across the country with frozen Persian food.

Before I would head home on each of my school breaks, a month or so out I would send emails to the folks I had made contact with professionally. Namely, the developers I had met before I left and other CEOs and business owners I felt would add value to my business. I would line up meetings throughout my week or sometimes two-week stay in Seattle. Each day I got up on my "school break," caught the bus from where I was staying in Kirkland and head to downtown Seattle in time for my meetings. At this point I wanted to keep those I admired in real estate development updated on my progress in school and with the business. I'd usually have 1 or 2 meetings a day and they would usually be early mornings. After my meetings, I would use the remainder of my day working on my business plan. With the gems I learned from my mentors and meetings, I would finesse my plan. I would apply their advice to what I was working on. Most of their advice at the time was "make sure you finish law school" and "don't take on too much." These were two very simple but sound pieces of advice.

Every time I would head back to school coming off break, there was always, and I mean always someone I had met that semester who did not come back. Any law school survivor will tell you, law school is brutal—I don't care what school you attend—and on top of that, I was trying to build a business at the same time. By the time I began law school, I had completed about the 20th draft of my business plan. And I had decided that it was time to pull the trigger on why I actually went to Grand Rapids. Yes, I aimed to obtain a law degree, but it was also the cheapest place in the country to buy an investment property. Knowing that I didn't have any money, I would have to be creative about how I would do so. The plan consisted of utilizing my financial aid money to buy a shanty ass duplex about 5 to 10 minutes from campus. I befriended a classmate who would be my first business partner—he pitched in money that he had saved up and we went into our first investment property together.

III. Near Death

Let's talk about lessons learned. Let's also set the stage. 2009 was a treacherous year economically for the U.S. and most of the global market. Foreclosures hit all-time U.S. records. When my law school business partner and I set our eyes on this two-story duplex in the Baxter neighborhood in Grand Rapids, Michigan, we had a vision to bring it back to life. At the time, the broker we were working with introduced us to a neighborhood contractor that would put small crews on investment properties for flips. The contractor wasn't technically legit—i.e., no license—but he had about 2 to 4 guys who did rehab work and even did some of the work himself. He was selling us on the idea that he could do the two-story renovation for $10,000 total! Initially I was skeptical, and then I was beyond skeptical. To try and ease our nerves, he took us on a short tour of homes he had renovated for between $10,000 and $20,000. Though my partner and I were both skeptical law students, we told ourselves that we would drive the work and ensure that we would keep costs down and meet our deadline. Our goal was to rent out both units in a month's time.

It was interesting how it all happened. During our torts class, we engaged in an offer battle with the bank because the duplex was an REO property. And this all transpired via text message no less! It was a foreclosed property and the bank was trying to get $20,000. We started at $9,000, and by the end of our 3-hour class, the bank accepted our offer of $13,000 for the two-story shit-hole of a duplex. Shit, you talk about being excited! I remember looking up at the classroom of about 40 to 50 students and thinking to myself, "No one has any idea what just happened. This is crazy, I just bought my first investment property." Now you're probably thinking, "Yeah, that's nice, but those students were paying attention and probably did well in that class." Yeah, well, I don't care about what you may think. But you should know I got out of that class with a solid B. Survival. I wasn't there to be top of my class in law school. If that was the case, I would have changed my plan accordingly. My goal was to learn as much as I could, survive the rigors of law school, and jumpstart my business. So, no, my grades weren't top-tier. But I'll tell you what. I never had to retake a class and I never failed a class. I got all my credits. And I was excited and proud to reach another milestone in my family—the youngest to buy a property, at 23 years old, and the youngest to buy an investment property, at 26 years old.

I worked out our investment numbers and knew that we could cash flow $1,200 a month. Split that in half and we each made $600. Again, I was carrying quite the financial load. I had a mortgage back home, living expenses, law school expenses, and rent in my current place. The rental income would cover my rent costs in Grand Rapids, which made my financial situation much more manageable. We decided to hire the so-called contractor to help us rehab/renovate the two story duplex. Everything started off great. The guy we hired brought in two to three of his people and they began an early demo, made the material purchases for new drywall, and went to work. We would check in daily with the contractor after our classes and show up on the jobsite to ensure our money was getting put to work.

One situation that stands out is when I started to get the feeling that something was wrong. I had shown up after classes to check in on the progress, and one of the laborers asked me for money. I believe it was something around twenty dollars or so. I remember telling him that he needed to wait until he got paid by "his boss" that was running the work. This guy was tall, slender, white, had teeth that were rotted or rotting, and didn't seem all there mentally. I remember looking at his shoes and they were so beat up and raggedy. I told him if he wanted to keep working on this project, he needed to get some steel-toed boots. He replied that he couldn't afford any at this time so I alerted my partner and we went out and bought him a pair of construction boots. I asked our contractor about him and he apologized for the incident and told me he would speak to him. I felt something wasn't right, but I didn't ask any more questions. As the weeks went on, the same guy who asked me for money wasn't showing up on the job. The contractor himself was starting to do the work, and the whole project moved slower. The contractor assured me that everything was OK and that the guy was going through some personal issues. When the guy did show up, though, he would continue to ask me for money. I couldn't take it anymore. I said, "What's the problem? Are you not getting paid? He said the contractor was paying him but that he was going through a financial hardship. I told him I was not going to pay him any additional money unless he was going to do more work.

I approached the contractor again and ask him, "What the fuck is up with your guy? Is he on drugs?" Come to find out . . . yes, he was addicted to crack (and no he wasn't black). So I'm thinking to myself, "Great. My first rehab project and I have a crackhead on my jobsite. It's one thing if he was going through rehab and making an effort to clean himself up, but instead he just showed up to get what he could, doing the bare minimum amount of work so that he could go out and get high. Needless to say, we told him he could not come back anymore. After that there was a snowball of fucked-up events. The contractor ended up losing his team and it was only him trying to show up and renovate a 2,000-square foot duplex by himself. Well, that put us way behind our schedule to collect rental income, so my partner and I had to jump in and do the work ourselves. But we could only do so much! We wouldn't dare touch the 100-year-old electrical system, so through the grapevine we found out about a head laborer and his crew. Let's just say, these cats reminded me of growing up in South Gate, Los Angeles—tats on their heads, they showed up in tank tops and dicky pants and while my partner and I buffed the 100-year old floors, the newly hired crew went to work on making sure we got electricity running through the duplex. Oddly enough, we were able to pre-lease both units. We took to Craigslist and had a good handful of people ready to rent.

The days were long. We showed up almost daily at the property to get dirty and put in some sweat equity. The 10k we had initially put into construction ended up being a total of 20k to get everything finished. My daily consisted of waking up, sitting in 3 to 6 hours of class, hit the library for another 5 to 8 hrs of studying, then to the property to complete the renovation. I'd get home close to midnight almost every night for that first semester of school. I know it sounds like a lot, and that's because it was. My motivation, beyond the long-term I describe in previous chapters, was food. I had already invested the little bit of money I had, and with the financial aid money I was supposed to use on food and shelter, I had now invested that in real estate, so I absolutely needed to get this property complete and rent-ready so I could feed myself. Throughout this process, there were nights where I would open my fridge and it would cough back at me because my fridge was starving!

I also remember calling one of my best friends, LaVance, and telling him how I was eating hard-boiled eggs for dinner and even he couldn't take it. He alerted a professor at Seattle University Law School, Hank McGee, concerning my situation. I knew Professor McGee well. He'd take me out to

lunch in Seattle and spit game to me about life. Next thing
I knew, a week later I received a check in the mail for $100.
Can't tell you how far I stretched that $100. About a month
later, the Breakfast Group, the local non-profit collective of
African American men in Seattle, sent me a check for $3,500.
I had been one of the group's youngest members when I lived
in Seattle. With this much-needed windfall, I was able to
get a bed, buy books, and cover rent until the next semester's
financial aid kicked in. I am forever grateful to the Breakfast
Group and their support.

Determined, we powered through the renovation. It
wasn't pretty, but it was a livable quarters and in line with
what was in the neighborhood—the heat worked, it had new
appliances, and we made a little breakfast bar and the families
we rented to were happy.

Like I said, we had a few different applicants to choose
from, but I decided that we should rent to people who
wouldn't normally get approved. I understood what it meant
to have shitty credit, and no job and being denied a place.
Shit, I've been denied a credit card and the Bon (now Macy's),
back in the day just trying to get a pair of socks. But I also
knew that having shitty credit didn't define me as a person. I
wanted to give people the opportunity to make things right
for themselves. We ended up renting both units with ease.
We took a risk and rented each unit to two separate families,
both on every social program you can think of. And one of
the families, neither mother or father had a job. They were
getting just enough unemployment to be able to afford rent.
Little did they know I was on the same social services they
were utilizing! But my thought process was and still is, if you
don't have a stable housing environment, seeking employment and obtaining an education will be hard to come by.
The downstairs family had 3 kids and the upstairs family had
2 kids. My criteria to them was clear: "As long as you pay rent
and keep the property clean, we wouldn't have a problem."
The families were grateful. As a first-year law student, I exe-

cuted my first lease as a landlord to an investment property. It was an exciting day for my partner and me. We collected security deposits, made copies of the lease, and celebrated with a cheap local six-pack.

We made it successfully to the other end! For the coming months, our tenants proved to us they could keep their word and they paid rent on time. Little did they know I desperately needed that income to keep me from losing my condo in Seattle and food in my fridge. Although I was in law school, I was scraping to get by. Like Outkast said referencing life, "me and you are neck to neck." But they saw me as their landlord and not as someone who was barely getting by financially.

I couldn't tell you the burden lifted off my shoulders once we were done renovating the duplex and had it rented. I could then focus on my legal studies. Yes, I had the occasional phone call from the tenants about minor things that needed to be touched up, but by that time we knew the right person to call to get it addressed. I can't lie—I had an extra bounce to my step whenever I would be on campus. In the words of the great Mac Dre, "I was in the building and I was feeling myself." But this extra step didn't last too long. Well, maybe about a year or so . . . that's until I brushed up against my first near-death experience.

I wasn't really close to dying but got-damnit it sure felt like it because I didn't see myself making it out of this one alive. I got a call around 2:30AM from the downstairs tenant. I had been dead sleep. He tells me the house is on fire. I don't hear him correctly, and I keep asking, "What do you mean? Stop joking with me, it's late." He replied, "There are fire trucks here, we're standing out in the rain and we don't have anywhere to go." I kept telling myself, this can't be. This is a nightmare, a terrible dream and I have to wake myself up. So I got up, put on some sweats, called a cab (this is pre-Uber days) and headed out to the property. It could not have been more dramatic. It was pouring rain at 3AM and fire trucks had blocked off the street. My first real estate deal is literally up in smoke in front of me. Standing on the curb were the two families—5 kids total—shivering in the cold. Rain dripped off their young faces. And their parents were livid! One of the fathers kept asking me, "Where are we supposed to stay?! Where are we supposed to stay?!" I couldn't get a handle on what was going on. I looked to my right and the roof was half-gone, half-charred.

The blaze had already been put out. The rain made a dashing sound as it hit the hot embers of the duplex; firemen were going in and out of the property. One of them asked who was the owner. I took a 7/11 big gulp and stated, "I'm the owner." I asked him what happened and he couldn't say. He mentioned that the electrical wiring in the attic may have been too hot and slow-cooked the installation until a fire ensued. I was in disbelief, and I was terrified, mortified. Meanwhile the parents were giving me an earful, asking me where they were supposed to stay because they had nowhere to go. Kids were crying, engines of the fire trucks were roaring, and I was feeling dizzy. Please God make me disappear! I've never in my life felt so helpless, small and insignificant AND responsible. I went from providing low-income families a place to get back on their feet, to right back on the streets. How the fuck did this happen? Within minutes, a news van had shown up, I knew then I had to split. I called my partner right away. He came, didn't even bother getting out of the car, and I jumped in and we peeled out.

Class was at 9AM.

Master Your Craft

"I got my start by giving myself a start"

—MADAME CJ WALKER

I. Stay in Your Lane

AS YOU CAN SEE FROM THE LAST CHAPTER, I HAD not yet mastered my craft (side eye). But I had not let that huge implosion of an effort define the rest of my dream to be a real estate developer and CEO. If anything, that tremendous learning lesson was a milestone for me as I began to master my craft to be a business mogul.

I felt like I got knocked the fuck out in a fight. You struggle to stand up, you're seeing double, then you lock your eyes on your opponent and you quickly have to make a decision. Most jump to the decision whether or not to continue the fight. For me it was not a decision whether to continue to fight, but more about HOW I was going to come back from adversity and win. It was never about whether or not I would continue the fight. Though, I must admit a small sense of doubt set in, I just never let it fester. (Fuck doubt.) There was nothing in this universe that would alter or deter my passion to be a real estate developer and business mogul. If I was going to survive, I would have to adapt. I would adapt to the bad times like I did the good times. Making adjustments is a crucial skill and this past experience sharpened exactly that. I

woke up standing at the proverbial fork in the road: one sign
read "Safety" and the other sign read "Live Life."

Staying in my lane meant that I kept to the original plan—
"stick to the script"—no matter the obstacle. My overall goal
was to be a savvy business mogul and real estate developer,
someone who garnered enough resources to effectively give
back to his community. But in order to get there I needed to
knock out a few tasks, like graduate from law school ☺. Ten
out of ten times, startups experience initial hardships and
those hardships serve as wind sails that can end up blowing
you off course. This happens to all of us; you get blown off
course because you:

1. Let doubt sink in;
2. Convince yourself that because you took an ass
    whooping, that direction was not meant for you (basi-
    cally #1);
3. Get sidetracked by the next shinier object; and / or
4. Switch careers/professions/aspirations for a per-
    ceived "easier" route.

Letting doubt sink in:
This fight against "doubt" is one of the toughest fights you'll
engage in, and not just as a business owner. This is a constant battle throughout life. While you cannot control outside forces, you can control who you want to become. Doubt
can be tricky and approach you from different angles. Here's
how to recognize it so you can thwart it.

It will come in the form of so-called friends. Get ready for
the people closest to you to lose faith. Some will experience
your failures with you but most will watch. They'll sideline
watch you through social media. You'll try and maintain your
personal status quo on social media. Don't do that. It will be
obvious to your audience that something's off. If you are one
to share every got-damn thing on your social media, use this
as an opportunity to be honest with your audience, but more

importantly be honest with yourself. Be real about the struggle you face. You'll want to be honest with yourself through whatever period of confusion, turmoil, or struggle. You'll want to do this for yourself. This does not mean you have to share every detail of your struggle, but when you experience doubt it will permeate through the other aspects of your life. You'll need to have your "day one's" in your corner. Your ride-or-die friends and family. Not watchers, but those on the ride with you. Lean on your support network for as much as you can. Take in as much advice, rest, and companionship that your network offers. You may not feel like going for a drink, a hike, or talking about your situation, but GO! You need to get your mind clear and the only way to do that is to wipe it clean with someone you love and experience a subtle moment where, temporarily you were able to escape doubt. You'll soon learn that if you are able to escape the grasp of "doubt," even for a fleeting moment, you can escape it anytime you want.

Convincing yourself that because you took an ass whooping that direction was not meant for you:
Smacked so hard you forgot your first name. You know what I'm talking about? Been through something so traumatic that you take an entirely new course? Like, "Welp, that shit wasn't for me, tried it, failed at it and moving on to the new new." More often than not, when we do not succeed at something we had set a goal to achieve, it can be the biggest blow to the ego. Let me ask you this, what is an ego, anyway? If you are so easily distracted from your passion because you took an ass whooping, than I would first say that you don't have much of an ego. Experiencing an ego blow during your initial start-up years are the most defining. You'll question yourself to the point where you will have convinced yourself that this path wasn't for you, and that you should explore another pathway to happiness and perceived success.

Adversity comes fast, and if you're a business owner it's going to come often. You have to get comfortable knowing that everyday will be a crap shoot. Yes, you should have a running to-do list, yes, you should have a schedule for how your day is going to go. But brass tax, your day is going to get fucked up. The universe is going to throw so many unknowns at you, your knees will buckle, tears will stream down your face, and you will question your very existence.

Do not forget—the question IS the fork in the road. This question, alone, is the first actionable step you'll take to going off course. You'll make a jolt of a turn, ill-prepared for what's to come next, down a lane you chose to go down because of external factors. Nothing innate in you forced you to make that decision. Think about the time and energy you invested in your idea; rather than help create that idea, you're starting down another road from scratch. And by the time you figure out the next thing you're going to do that's going to make money, you could have been leaps and bounds down the road with your passion. A new lane requires new information, new networks, new goals, and most of all, it requires shitty days of regret. Long story short, it's ok to take ego blows. It humbles you. Humble yourself. Stay on the path, no switch up, ok? Taking an "L" does not speak to whether or not this is the right path for you. Conversely, it speaks to how creative you're going to be to come out on top after going through it. "Tough times don't last, tough people do."

Getting sidetracked by the next shinier object:
Boy is it easy to get distracted these days but when you're feeling down and out, it's so much easier to lose focus. And know that vultures are there waiting to prey on you. They are waiting for your hopelessness. Like the US military to poor families. They feed off of it. Some of these vultures disguise themselves as the US military, Pyramid marketing schemes (Amway, among others), and old bosses. Other times, you'll feel the urge to follow an economic trend. Right now, real estate is hot in Seattle, and all of a sudden everyone and their momma wants to be a real estate agent. They learn that the

bar of entry is really low. Instead of following their passion, they get caught like a deer in headlights at what seems to be an oasis of financial freedom. Don't chase money, unless money is your passion. Believe me, I love money but I don't chase it. Remember, it gets printed everyday.

Switching careers/professions/aspirations for a perceived "easier" route:
If you truly are looking to start a business, you must state your timeline. When you first register your business with the state, you typically have to let the state know how long you want to be in business. This is done within your articles of incorporation. They ask to state either a number of years, or you can select "perpetual." Perpetual is the long haul. Selecting this timeline as a business model means there is no end date. At least, not one you have in mind.

In your business plan you should outline and clearly define how long you want to be in business. Is it 2 years? 5 years? 10 years? Although this timeline seems arbitrary at first, it's the first line of defense when you feel the urge to switch up and give up on the business for some other career, profession or aspiration. This is all a build up. If either the first, second, or third pitfalls mentioned above take root in your mind, you will switch your career. You will abandon the plan because you let doubt win. Sometimes it's circumstances, you know? And that's real. Maybe you just learned the news you have a baby on the way? Maybe you fell head over heels for someone and wedding plans are in the works? Or maybe you just got too scared? Your resolve will be tested. Because unless you got automatic funds you'll be tempted to find another career or profession that yields the amount of dough it's going to take to finance that unexpected life circumstance.

When it comes to your aspirations. You had them at first, right? You know, when you first started the company. You had dreams and aspirations to change the world with your app, product or service. You aspired to be the best. You aspired to have the world acknowledge you because you knew that they were missing you. They were missing your tech wiz, they were missing your creativity, they were missing your genius. You were on the margins and you aspired to show them that they should have never overlooked you! Where'd that go? Huh? Where'd that go? Circumstances and money forced the switch up? What has doubt forced you to aspire to now? What has your changed life circumstance forced you to aspire to now? How many times are you going to switch up your flow? Nah, you didn't really want it. You weren't ready for the grind. You let outside forces control your destiny and determine your fate. Maybe you don't care. Maybe the change is what it is and you're going to keep it pushing on the new journey. If that's the case, stop reading—put this book down and get back to your newfound career. This book ain't for you. This book is for the hardcore hustlers. The muthafucka who's going to do everything in their power to get over that hurdle, knock down that brick wall, and get whatever they know is theirs. The hustle by nature isn't supposed to be easy; that's why they call it a hustle. If you're stronger than Darwinism, this world is yours. Your dreams are yours. You get blown off course, watch that dream wither away year after year. I'm not writing this book to be nice about how to maintain your business and chase your dream. Total opposite. Force is met with force. If you're really about your startup or continuing the business you started, you're not going to let marriage get in the way, you're not going to let a baby get in the way. You're not going to let someone not hiring you deter you. If you're a true hustler, you're going to let those things motivate you even more. You're going to let those changes in life circumstances fuel you even more. It's going to be a jetpack. BLAST OFF!

II. Who's Stopping You?

The fight to NOT want to live a life of regret also has a dark side. Some people call it FOMO (Fear Of Missing Out),

I call it "confused ass muthafuckas." Striving for your goal can sometimes blind you. Your urge for success gets hoe'd out. You start to reach for things that aren't there. Forced mirages and "perception is reality" are fucked up, temporary, shit-stained dreams. Your lane may hit traffic, be bump and go while everyone else is blazing by you doing whatever it is they are doing. You start to ask questions: "What is it that she's doing?" "What is it that he's doing?" "How do I get in that lane and move as fast as them?" You begin to spend time investigating why that person is moving so fast. You start to subconsciously measure yourself against someone and something that has nothing to do with your mission, goals, or vision.

Social media has given us supreme and ultimate access into some of the most intimate and personal moments of success of individuals and those considered "famous." Can you believe it? There's an actual term coined, "Instagram model"? Whether you like it or not, the world is moving fast and it doesn't need big companies validating your entrance to play that game. The power is actually at our fingertips. With that power—I'm able to edit this page in a bar listening to Ginuwine with ratchets looking for attention—what are you choosing to do with it? What are you choosing to share? Bigger than that, who the hell are you following? And why are you following them? Are you just 1 of 111 million of Kim Kardashian's sheep? Take a look at what/who you are choosing to follow and how that is directly correlated to your success as an aspiring entrepreneur. Are you chasing followers? Are you chasing likes? Is that validating you and your dreams? You got to be on your own terms. You can't let that social media shit influence you. One of my best friends had a great quote. I asked him why he thought people post some of the most ridiculous shit (at least what we would consider ridiculous) and he replied, "People move to LA and New York to chase likes on the 'gram." I don't know why that hit me like a ton of bricks.

As I think more about it, I was in awe. I was in awe that people's perceived vision of success involves relocating to another city just for what they can post on social media. Now, that's not the obvious reason why they are moving, but their subconscious has been so worn down by the flood of images that they make up an excuse to move. Not to say there are not valid reasons to relocate your life. That's not what I'm getting at with this moment of constructive criticism. Rather, think more about your choices and "why" you're choosing them. Think about what you are allowing in your daily feed and think about how that might influence you in ways that— without you knowing—is pulling your true self and your true identity to pieces. Soon, you'll look like everyone else, dress like everyone else, eat like everyone else, work out like everyone else, and you'll become just another someone else.

Master your craft, make mistakes, fuck "likes," and push out a work product. Ain't that "the pot calling the kettle black," you might be saying. Oh yes, my social media be poppin'. It's all strategic and I put in that work for real. Pull my card any day, sucka MC. Who's stopping you? Who's stopping you from curating your best life? Who's stopping you from posting whatever you want. Keep it authentically you. It's not about the "likes," it's not about the comments— it's about your reach. Who are you reaching? How far does your reach go?

The answer is no one is stopping you. You have been blessed and given every tool you need to accomplish every dream you could have on this earth. The only thing that's stopping you is your lack of persistence, your lack of dedication, your lack of understanding your self-worth, and saying FUCK THAT! FUCK societal rules. Entrepreneurs—real ones, and you are a real one right?—they have no rules. The only rules an entrepreneur has are the rules they create. So . . . who's stopping you?

Streets is Watching

"You are what you share"

—ANONYMOUS

I. Social Media

'M ONLY WRITING THIS CHAPTER FOR THOSE WHO actually care about their reputation, business and personal. I'm not writing this to help you create the perfect social media persona but I do know a couple things. My engagements are up and I'm getting checks off the social media. I'd rather have a couple thousand quality followers with a five to ten percent conversion rate than millions of fake followers and no close rate. There are full books written solely on this topic and I simply won't do it justice here. I'm actually not trying to, so before I get into why I believe social media is important beyond the obvious reasons, I want to dig into a few specifics about the essentials of social media and how I have been able to "leverage" this tool to not only build my brand but build my business. I should say, however, that what's obvious to some isn't obvious to others. With that said, the two most obvious reasons most people understand why social media is important is (1) it's free, and (2) you control it.

Quick disclaimer: I call these two reasons "obvious" but I have to reiterate (as I watch most people's Twitter and Facebook feeds) that just because something is free and under your control doesn't necessarily mean you are using it properly. I have to cover my mouth most times because I gasp every time I log on to a social media platform. Sitting here sipping on a cup of Persian tea like, "Did he or she really just post that? Do they really give no fucks?" I don't know about you but I'm out here watching people destroy their own brand and reputation daily with some weird, sideways, too much information, negative-ass posts.

#1 Keep it positive.
Jesus! For the love of God, keep your shit positive! If you're wondering why no one is in your inboxes giving you business or inquiring about your business that might be because your posts are negative as all hell. There is a very simple theory I live by and one I truly believe: The energy you put out is the same energy you're going to get back. With that said, if your posts repetitively talk about how bad your day was or how things are not going your way, what kind of energy do you expect to get back? You took time out of your day to spew negativity when (under your control) you could have easily not have posted at all, or at least spin it into a positive. Yes, you'll get a litany of condolence comments. Don't do it for that temporary satisfaction. Despite a Facebook friend commenting, "wishing you the best through these tough times" and "we are here for you", what's most important—and I can almost guarantee—is that they are typing one thing but in their head they are thinking: "What the fuck is going on and why are they sharing this?" So, I would suggest this: before you act on the urge to share about your negative experience, think about how you can take that negative experience and turn it into a positive post. Understand this, every post, every single post, counts. It's on the inter webs, it's stuck there forever. Here's an example:

Negative post: "I hate how the city has so much traffic now. So many people moving here, it's so annoying!"

Positive post: "I've noticed there have been more and more cars on the road. Man, it can be annoying sitting in traffic but at the same time it's giving me time to think and reflect on a lot of things going on in my life. Low-key thankful."

#2 Do not overshare.
If I see another post about someone telling all their business about their relationship with their significant other and how they got cheated on or how they are not giving them any attention or spews hateful words towards a family, friend, or boss, talking about how they hate their job . . . I'm going to do absolutely nothing other than shake my head as I read the post and judge you. LMAO!

Although whatever is happening in your life is important to you, keep in mind that oversharing takes away all the mystique and wonder. People don't need to inquire about you, your personal life, or more specifically your business because you're telling them too much and you're actually helping them come to their own conclusion to *not* contact you. Make them curious. Don't overshare.

#3 Be strategic about personal and business posts (keep it relatable).
Let's dice this pineapple: There's a balance between what you share about what's "positively" happening in your personal life and being too business-oriented. You can turn people off by being too professional. Because social media has allowed people to share any and everything, that's what people expect. Don't give them what's expected. Give them a balance of both. How do you balance? It's going to be different for everyone. At the end of the day people want to interact with a real person and not a robot. Your followers want to know you're real, have a personality (one they can relate to) and

you can do that by mixing in personal posts that won't damage your reputation or image. My rule of thumb: I keep my family and my intimate/personal relationships out of social media. On rare occasions I'll share that part of my life, but very rarely.

My strategy may not work for you. It may work in your favor to share what I don't. That's what you're going to need to do homework on. If you have a daycare company and you're looking to add more families to your client list, then you may want to share how well and stable your own home life is in order to provide comfort for that type of clientele. What you share about personal and business is going to be dependent on your type of business. I created my own rules to the social media game. I would recommend you do the same and stick to it and find that balance.

#4 Don't give in to others.

This one is super personal for me. I've had plenty of people ask why I don't share them on social media or why I haven't responded to their friend request. Here's why I have a "no family or intimate partner" rule on social media: I want to maintain some sort of privacy. And second, my family is my family, my partner is my partner, not for thousands of others to know about just because they want to be nosey. I'm not sharing what's most sacred to me with strangers. Just how I feel. Last, if I didn't respond to a friend request, it's pretty simple, I don't want you in my shit. Nothing personal, just don't. So don't budge or give in if you have your social media rules. You want to feel good and not regretful about your social media.

#5 Take criticism and build off of it.

If people are saying great things about your social media presence, double down on that! If people are not saying anything about it (which most will do if they have nothing positive to say), then ask them. Get their feedback, track that feedback, and make the necessary adjustments.

#6 Take strategic risks!

Don't be afraid to try new things! Switch it up a bit. Share different parts of your personality via gifs, articles, emojis, pictures and stories. See what sticks with people and generates the most engagement and double down on that!

#7 Watch who's watching you.

Make sure you are scanning your latest followers. You want people following you who you are targeting. It may feel good to wake up and have 10 new friend requests on FB but if those 10 people can't help you grow your business, give you business, or find you business, what does that say about how you've branded and marketed yourself? Work on attracting the right audience, watch them, and interact with them. Last, the of majority people don't interact on social media, they lurk and watch your posts. Remember, just because they don't "like" or "comment" doesn't mean they didn't see it or were not affected by your post. They are sitting back, sipping their tea, scoping your movements. Watch the ones that can make a difference for you and your business.

#8 Every once in awhile, give no fucks.

Every once in awhile I would say it's ok to show a vulnerable side and drop a real post that my not be so serious. Just don't do it all the time. It lets people know you're human and gives them a personality to relate to but more importantly give no fucks once in awhile and just be authentically you! We all need a break. Fake it 'til you make it isn't really a thing, so keep it real.

II. Memberships & Affiliations

No matter what you do you're going to have haters. So it's ever more important that you have a strong exterior village that will be there to support your mission and moves. This means affiliating. You want to look for groups who are directly in line with your type of business and within your business sector. I first suggest exploring your city's Chamber of Commerce; every city has one. They are a hub and business organization that is in place to support all business. If your chamber is strong I suggest joining. This will get you access to other companies and is an easy place to begin building relationships. They'll have networking events, panel discussions, and various opportunities to meet other like-minded business folks, as well as established business professionals and entrepreneurs. Again, like I said if they are strong, they'll have a list of numerous events happening every month. Pick and choose which events are the ones that will most benefit you.

Next you'll want to find groups and organizations that specifically are there to support your industry and sector. You will see more impact and results from these organizations as they are specific to how you will grow your business. You will find people who will be clients. You will find people from whom you will seek services and you'll find people who are just good people with whom to build professional relationships in that group.

Here's the caveat: You cannot expect your business to grow in any way if you are not active with your membership. Think about your paid membership in terms of an investment. If you think paying your membership dues and not being an active member is going to grow your business, you are completely wrong. You need to be active. Hit the happy hour events, hit the serious panel discussions. Hit the annual meetings. Make an effort. You'll see the same people over and over again and a level of trust will emerge. And let's be real, if you have no trust, you have no business. You cannot and will not build trust by being a paid member only. Get your ass out there and pound the pavement; foster those relationships. You only get what you put into it and if you're a small start up, all expenses are crucial so why not make the most out of it? Plus, there are typically free food and drinks at those events. If you're struggling, what's your excuse? Affiliate and foster trust. This is the hustle.

Last, becoming a paid member is not just an investment. It's also how you market and brand your company. Every time you show up and hand out those business cards you're marketing and branding yourself. What are you wearing? How are you representing your company? Do you have your elevator pitch down? Did you forget your cards? These membership events are a really great and easy way to get your name out there. Note: It won't happen overnight. I suggest you find your top two or three groups and focus on those. Attend as much as you can, involve yourself. Get on a committee, join the board, be active. Again, you are investing in marketing yourself. It may take a year (or a few years) until you began to see the yield. Ultimately, if you able to come away with checks from those groups and those checks are more than your membership dues, then I'd say that's a worthy investment. That's why you do it! Be patient. Patience in these spaces is key. If you're frustrated that you're not coming away with any business, then instead of blaming the organization or the people in it, take a look at yourself. Do people know what it is you do or even what you're selling? If they don't, then how do you expect them to call you for business? If you're a new business, make sure your elevator pitch is the same, every single time. You have to pound it in people's head. Streets are watching. Give them something to watch but remember consistency is key.

If you can sell yourself, then your products and services will come next. At the same time you are building your reputation. The streets are watching! When you show up, know that people are watching you. Just because they are not looking directly at you does not mean they are not watching. Come prepared and come hungry.

III. Your Business Brand

Branding, one of the most important pieces to the game. Branding is more than just a logo and the name of your company. Although, I'll discuss the importance and strategy to a logo and company name, I want to first dig into your brand. What does your brand stands for? What does it mean? Where did it come from?

I must admit I made the mistake of almost crossing wires too early. As a matter of fact, "almost" is not the word. I "did" cross branding wires too soon. How? Well, most people are familiar with Onpoint Real Estate Services as my company name, a full-service real estate company. But Onpoint did not get founded until December of 2012 in my living-room office. Prior to that I started GardnerGlobal, Inc. (GG). In 2009, every email I sent out, my business cards, and the website was all branded (GG). So when I started Onpoint Real Estate in 2012, as you can imagine people were confused. For three years I was branding GG as a real estate development and investment company and then all of a sudden a new logo and new company name came from me all across my social and email blasts. I had to make the switch in regards to the branding and knew it was going to be a big push, but I continued to push Onpoint until it began to register.

In my case, GardnerGlobal, Inc. is my parent company that allows me to bring on investors. Deeper than that, I studied Warren Buffet's business model and the models of my mentors and realized they shared key similarities. I liked their business models and so I wanted to pursue building it for myself. I wanted to build a parent company who had a singular purpose to own assets, whether businesses or real estate. Keeping it simple, I just wanted to own shit, and GardnerGlobal, Inc. was my vehicle to do so. So how does that parlay into branding? Like I mentioned above, I branded my company to be a development company but I had to pivot. Pivot in the direction of now branding brokerage services and property management services, and all while doing so under a different company name. This, my friends, was no easy task. To this day I think people are still confused.

I had to make the pivot because I had no money to start

developing or acquiring real estate. I had to either find investors who would allow me to invest their money in real estate or I had to go out and build that money pile for myself. After I took on four early seed investors, I realized two things: (1) at that time my circle/peers/friends/family did not have disposable income to invest, and (2) asking people to invest in my dream was like pounding my head against a brick wall. I pulled back and decided that I would start managing property. Through property management, I would touch numerous clients, build a residual income and cash flow, build my reserves to develop, and most importantly build my brand.

What does building a brand mean? For me, building a brand was building trust. Not just with potential clients or folks who I wanted to do business with. My net extended much farther than that. My brand of trust should resonate with those who may never use my real estate services. This is extremely important to me because although they won't necessarily be using my services, they will be the people who will speak about your name or company when you're not there. I'm no one to tell you what to be concerned with, but for me I'm more concerned with what people say about my company and me, for that matter, when I'm not around. And although they've never done business with you, your personal brand should carry positive vibes (more about this in the next sub-chapter). Even though I felt I did a good job of managing my personal brand, people were still confused about my business brand. How did I know they were confused? I would get the same question over and over again. "What do you do?" "Are you a broker?" "What kind of real estate are you in?" A sign of a solid brand is when those questions are eliminated and the questions then become, "How can I refer you business?" Or they are asking specific questions related to your product or service. But people didn't know what my services *were* to refer me or to ask about them. No bueno! I had to build a new website, decide on a new logo, create a new slogan, implement company

values, the whole nine! I don't recommend taking this route
unless you're intentional about it.

IV. Your Personal Brand

If you have Instagram, then you should know how important it is to maintain a personal brand. Social media has done a couple things to our culture, I believe. It has allowed for over sharing of personal information, and created addictive phone use. Knowing these things, how are *you* leveraging social media to build *your* personal brand? You can try and separate yourself from your business all you want, but the two are inextricably linked. Your personal brand in many ways becomes your business brand. Your values, your philosophy, your style, and all the way down to the food you eat. You are presenting a lifestyle. Whatever that lifestyle is, you are deciding to share it with the world.

People are going to see your lifestyle and they are going to decide if they either want to get to know you more, or not. People will watch your Snapchat and Instagram stories and they'll sit back and judge. It's the reality. So, give them something to judge. If you are selling a product, post yourself using your product, post others using your product. Incorporate your product into your lifestyle. People have a lifestyle in mind, so give them something to use. The same goes with services. Document people using your services and place yourself in the middle of that transaction. You can sell your audience without hard-selling them and asking them to buy from you. I feel as though most people don't like being hard-sold anyway. In the early stages of your company, you are the company; so while your personal brand is tied to your business brand, use it wisely.

1. Don't overshare.
2. Hashtag your slogan or company name in your posts.
3. Be repetitive.
4. Be consistent.

If you have the resources you should consider hiring a social media specialist. This specialist needs to know you enough to be able to capture your voice. Hiring someone can save you an immense amount of time. Yet and still ensure that your social media team or consultant understands the above basic rules—it is true, in this day and age, you are what you post. So make it count.

Desire, Dedication, Discipline

"Appear weak when you are strong, and strong when you are weak"

—SUN TZU

I. Unrelenting

THIS CHAPTER WAS NAMED FOR THREE WORDS THAT guided four years of my life and every day since. From fourteen to eighteen years old, in the wrestling room at John F. Kennedy High School. I would see these words inscribed in big bold red letters every day on the grey cinder block wall in the gymnasium behind the bleachers. *Desire, dedication, discipline.* Little did I know at age 14 that these words would be core values that keep me focused and working at a relentless pace. (Shout out to Coach Kostecka) Along with these words was a phrase that my step-mother embedded in my brain simultaneously. I can't remember if I was a freshman or sophomore but she made a collage of pictures of the family with several inspirational quotes, some printed and some hand-written with purposely charred edges. Dead center of the collage was the quote "Believe In Yourself." Twenty years later this quote would be my daily mantra. Of course I thought I came up with it out of the blue when I began hash tagging all my social media, then my step-mom brought over the collage she had made from home and there it was, Believe In Yourself—I credit her for planting that seed. Don't take for granted the power that words can have on your mentality. The same way words can make you feel shitty is the same way they can make you feel confident.

Desire

I was blessed to move up to Seattle and have a moral support network with my Dad and Stepmom. It was reinforced every time I sold myself short, whether with grades, sports, or home life. They never allowed me to take a shortcut. However, there is more to the story. While growing up in South Gate, California, my grandparents raised my sister and me. I was nine years old when my biological mother couldn't carry the weight of two kids in addition to her precarious balance with addictions to alcohol, drugs, and the party life. Needless to say, I was an angry child and an angry young adult. I have since learned how to deal with those emotions (Ha! Who am I kidding?). I may criticize her but the hardest and least celebrated thing she did was walk up to my grandparents doorstep and give them custody of my sister and me—she kept us out of the state system and made sure that we were never separated.

Why am I telling you this? Is this going to be another rags to riches sob story? No, it's not. Sadly, my story is far more common than it should be . Millions of African-American kids, especially those born in the 80s, share my story. But it's what I did with my humble beginnings that gives people pause. At an early age, I always felt I was different than other kids at school. My mother tells this story (before she turned us over to my grandparents) about a time we went to Silver Lake Park in Los Angeles. My step-father was on the court playing basketball, my mother was entertaining my sister on the swing set, and the other park kids were throwing a football or playing tag. While with my sister, my mother looks up for me and sees me perched up on a park bench with a newspaper in my hands looking like a fifty-year-old scanning the business page. I was just seven or eight. She said after that she knew there was something different about me. Maybe it's nothing that different at all. Maybe it just means I'm a nerd? In either case, I was always one to slow down my environment, assess and plot how I would interact with it. I was bored easily. I'd rather read the newspaper at age seven than play with the neighborhood kids.

Fast forward to my early years of elementary and junior high school when I lived with my grandparents: South Gate, California. A city of 96,000 people and damn near everyone of them was Latino. I grew up a minority amongst minorities—crabs in the Los Angeles barrel. I was typically the only Black kid in all my classes. Although there were a few other Black kids, there were too few of us to form any type of contingent. I went to South Gate Junior High, and between 1995 and 1997, it was considered the largest junior high in the nation by population. Any smart parent most likely knows that this is not a statistic to be particularly proud of considering the normal class size ranged from thirty to forty students. My school had scant resources and I spent most of the time thinking about surviving the day and getting home without getting my ass whooped or worse, shanked.

I would get made fun of when I would come home from school and play with the neighborhood kids. My grandparents raised my sister and I off a fixed income, social security, and a small pension. I didn't have street/casual or professional clothes. I did, however, have a school uniform (blue slacks with a white polo) that I wore everyday to school and to kick-it because I lacked other clothes, so I would hit the street in my uniform pants. I would at least change my shirt.

I would change out the white polo, cut the sides of the pants and hit the block. I remember the sinking feeling of getting clowned by the other neighborhood kids because I would come out to play with them in my school uniform pants. Living with my grandparents, I never had name-brand shoes. We would shop at Payless. The pressure I would feel every day to keep up and compete materially with the other kids was a feeling of ultimate helplessness. One day I made some money from washing cars in the neighborhood and put it together with my neighborhood best friend, Eddie. We hit the second-hand store on Long Beach Boulevard and bought some overalls and a couple shirts. We would share these clothes and trade days for who was wearing what.

I remember the times when my grandma would make dinner, and after we ate I would still be terribly hungry. A salad and one box of hamburger helper for four people only goes so far. Thank goodness for my neighbors, Javier and Diane, who would always let me and my sister come over and eat their food. They never once complained or made us feel less than. They always opened their home to us when we were hungry. If you've ever gone to bed hungry, you know first-hand the trauma that causes. My ego, my pride, my confidence . . . everything took the blow. These were the early seeds that sparked my desire to be who I am today and who I will become in the future. There was nothing I could do from 9 to 14 to change my situation: I had a party driven, drug-addicted mother, and a father who battled drugs in his own right and lived out of state. In this area of LA, every block was a territory for a certain gang. And at school, every part of the blacktop was a territory for a certain gang. In classrooms I sat next to cholos with tatts on their skulls and girls who showed up to school pregnant at 12 or 13 years old. My place of public education had more similarities with prison than differences. This was my concrete jungle.

I offer this background to set the stage for why having desire is an essential when embarking on your journey as an entrepreneur. For everyone, it will be a different experience or reason. For me, starting a business was more than just real estate and developing buildings, it was making sure that the cycle I went through with my family NEVER happened again. My focal point was rooted in my desire to not be poor (not just monetarily but mentally), to not have to wear the same clothes every damn day or share clothes, and to be able to enjoy the small things in life and to provide (for) my entire family I wanted to be an "earner"—earn everything so no one could take it away!

This desire is an important attribute to name because there will be times when you feel like quitting. There will be times when you will let your environment dictate your future and you're going to need a tank full of desire to keep going. You are going to be confronted with challenges you have not seen before. You are going to be challenged every single day and your desire, your reasoning for doing what you do (separate from passion) will keep you going. Maybe it's not hunger for you, but whatever your struggle was or is, leverage that and remind yourself constantly of those arduous times. Equally important is to not forget what it is you want. What fuels your desire and what it is you desire are two separate things. I gave you only a snippet of one struggle that affected me. It helped paint the picture of what it is that I want. That strong desire to take care of my family in every aspect is my driver. Find yours. It's closer than you think. And if you have found that desire, do not let it go. When that desire flame goes weak, think about those times when you had your confidence killed and how you survived, and how you never want to go back. I'm never going back, ever, and neither should you. Tough times don't last. Tough people do.

Dedication

How dedicated are you to this new venture/business? What does dedication mean to you? Have you ever been dedicated to anything/anyone? If the answer is no, then why not?

Are you scared to be dedicated to something/someone? If so, where does that fear come from? Do you know? I don't mean to sound like a damn psychiatrist but I'm asking these questions so you can reflect on the depth of what it means to be dedicated. I would assume when you use this word in the context of marriage, life partner, or kids, you would have a better sense of what it means? If you are serious about your new venture, then you must have the same level of dedication, if not more. You must be dedicated to the mission (that you created) and honest about the work you are putting in to see it grow and prosper. And don't forget, dedication is something that life tests on a daily basis. With each test and with each moment(s) of adversity your dedication will be one of the essentials that must remain planted and firm. How to stay firm? Remember, this is business. As one of my mentors said to me, "You'll need to have ice in your veins." Truer words were never spoken.

For myself, I'm not an outwardly emotional person, but I internalize a lot. I also know that I have a tendency to react off of emotion quite immediately. This is not something you want to practice. Whenever someone "steals" a deal from you, speaks terribly about you behind your back, tries to demoralize you publicly or is just a flat-out hater, this is when you must keep firm. Remind yourself that the only reason they are even mentioning your name is because they are threatened by your future success.

With this being said, you must understand that dedication actually means "doing the work." Making time to do the work is the lynchpin to your new company. Excuses on why you didn't complete a task will hurt your growth more than you think. The smallest task, the most miniscule of things you'll need to get done will be the one crutch that will be sure to have you limping into your future. In particular, procrastination will destroy your new business. People are creatures of habit. If procrastination is one of them, get rid of it quickly. How to do this? Block out times in your calendar—whether

writing it down or electronically, you need to be able to have
that time dedicated to completing the tasks that are essential
to growing your business.

Discipline

If dedication is "doing the work", then discipline is "making
time" to do the work. There is nothing my team members
do on a daily basis that I have not done myself. Especially
at the early stages, I maintained the social media, handled
business development, maintained our website, created the
filing system, fielded phone calls, answered emails, learned
our property management software, planned and conducted
home showings, created Craigslist ads for our rentals, dealt
with upset tenants, fixed garbage disposals, and the list keeps
going. Since I have touched every aspect of the company, I
know intricately how every part of the company works.

When there are kinks in any one of these components,
you will need to know how it works and you'll need to know
how to fix it.

Money's Funny, But it Ain't a Joke

"I had crossed the line.
I was free; but there was
no one to welcome me to
the land of freedom. I was
a stranger in a strange land"

—HARRIET TUBMAN

I. Skin in the Game

WHEN I SAY MONEY'S FUNNY, WHAT I'M TALKING about is it might be the funniest thing on this planet. Money is the only thing that changes people within seconds of them knowing you have it, and it's the only thing that changes people within seconds of them knowing you don't have it. And that to me is the joke—the fact that we put a printed piece of paper ahead of human needs is, at times, hilarious. Even more striking is how we've been fooled to think that money is the purveyor of thoughts (education), the driver of economics (work), and a system of belief (religion). For example, let's be real, the Catholic Church doesn't respect religion. They respect currency. In all

forms. "praise be to the almighty dollar" Third Eye Blind.
So with that being said, let's talk about how you're going to finance your business within this structure.

In the United States of America, you may come from a community that is blessed with not having to come to this country forcibly. In other words, you are not a descendant of slavery. Your lineage wasn't raped and forced to work for free to benefit an entire race of people on several continents. You may come from a community that has been blessed by those who have had to come here forcibly. These same crucibles have been the thought-leaders in ensuring that not only their rights but the rights of everyone who is not white and who has not felt the boot of oppression has the equity to live life through the basic god-given (universal) rights that have been bestowed since birth. What isn't god-given when you're born is money 💔.

There is no magic number for how much you'll need to initially finance your business. Whatever you think it's going to cost, double it. There are so many unknowns, and those unknowns will cost. Unless you have had the experience of working in a job where you've launched a business directly correlated with what your entrepreneur vision is, be prepared to pay for those learning lessons. Even then at your most experienced level, when you go at it alone and you no longer are a W2 employee, there will be many unanticipated costs.

My perspective on financing your company comes from a paradigm and a reality founded in pure struggle and grit. If you're looking to get the play-by-play on how to do several rounds of raises through angel investors, convertible notes, and series A and B raises, well then, you'll need to look elsewhere. I wasn't taught any of that. Nor did I have family who were entrepreneurs in my lifetime to teach me, let alone family who were lawyers and accountants and could teach this kid how to play the game of capitalism. So I've learned to look at actions, not words; they want to tell you that this game is a great game to play. But take it from me, it's not so fun when you don't know the rules. And don't think that when you've learned the rules that you've learned ALL the rules. The rules change, the rules shift, locally, regionally, and globally. Unless you are the one creating the rules, buckle your ass up and be prepared to come out of pocket because financing your business is going to be like this Norwegian airline I'm taking to Prague—terrible.

Look no further than family and friends. This may be a cliche statement when it comes to the start-up community. But it's true! The ones closest to you, the ones who know you—who know your grit, your hustle, your determination and have seen you turn water into wine growing up—are the ones who are going to be there as your initial financial supporters.

Why will they be the first ones to support? They'll support you because they are familiar with you know how much skin you've put in the game. They will have heard you at family dinners talking about how you wanted to start a business. They will have seen your initial drawings as you sketched and scribbled out a potential logo of your company, even on a paper napkin years ago. They will have already seen your dream. But most importantly, they will have been the first people you call when you've had a tough day and things didn't go your way. They are the folks who kept you going and continually watched you—time and time again—shave off your skin for this dream. These people will have been the ones who've told you, "You're crazy" but admire you behind closed doors. These are the people who have seen and felt the unending belief in yourself to make your dream a reality. These are your first contributors.

Don't get it twisted, they are not going to contribute based off the sole purpose that they've witnessed you work hard. You will need empirical data—however much you have—that shows "something" about what your business can do. This is where your business plan comes in handy. You need to have a plan and the plan needs to be so tight that you don't even need to send them a Word document. It is your thirty-second elevator speech. It's ingrained in your bone marrow. There should be no need to reference your plan when speaking about it because you know it inside and out. That's your initial skin in the game. Regardless of what someone thinks, if you have taken the time to write out a thoughtful game plan for your business, they'll respect real work when they see it. More importantly, they respect real vision.

Now, you must execute on that vision. Not several visions but a singular vision. Your language must stay consistent with your vision and your day-to-day deliverables and executables. Ready for the tough part? Time. The only real skin in the game that one can calculate, measure and speak on, is time. Yes you will need some seed capital to get things going. But this book isn't for the entrepreneur whose family can lace them with their first 50k or 300k to start their business, à la Mr. Jeff Bezos. This is for the person who has nothing to start with but a few thousand in the bank they've been able to luckily save over a few tedious years. Yes, this is for you. And know that it's not about money, it's about how you use it. Take whatever you have saved and deposit it into your dream bank account. It's an account only you have access to and it's an account only you can grow or you can lose. I've heard a few different approaches to managing money. Old school: Save, save, save. New School: Make your money work for you! Dame Dash had some interesting things to say on this topic. He said he doesn't save money. As soon as he gets it, he's reinvesting it into another project. He understands that money is a tool. What good is a hammer if it's sitting in your garage in the toolbox not getting used? Money is meant to create opportunities and if it's sitting in your bank doing nothing like the hammer in the toolbox, then you can't expect much from it.

Right now, I know what you're telling yourself, "But Jaebadiah, if you don't save for a rainy day, then you'll have no safety net to fall back on." My response to that mindset is simple: Then you're not an entrepreneur. We take risks because we believe. And that belief is stronger than worrying about some temporary-ass safety net that will eventually break because it can't hold all the weight of your self-doubts. The time it will take you questioning yourself and casting negative energy on your next move is time you can spend being optimistic and solution-oriented. Which one do you choose? I choose the latter. Yes, you will need actual money to start your business, but that's not the ONLY thing you need. Do not let the absence of money be the reason you do not pursue your dream. "FUCK MONEY" was a phrase that became all too common with someone I loved dearly. Her family would randomly yell it out when the topic of money would come up, and though it was funny and made for a hilarious laugh, it was also true. FUCK MONEY. Like, literally, fuck it. That's what it's there for. It's not concerned about you, so don't be bothered by it. Be ingenious. Be forward-thinking. Push yourself to make the most with the least. You don't need the most. You just need your passion, dedication, and resilience.

II. Lean and Mean (bootstrapping)

When it comes to financing your business, take the peanuts you have saved and test yourself. See how far you can make it stretch before you go out for a capital raise. Include in your plan a budget for what those peanuts can accomplish. It will get you to a certain point. Acquire certain company assets, whether it's an updated website, a new logo, or a piece of equipment or inventory that is dire to your start-up. When stretching your initial start-up funds, really, really stretch it. What I mean by that is don't pay for things at face value. If you need a website and you got three quotes for cost, rethink paying for the cheapest one just to have something online. If you find quality in the higher quote, then go with the higher quote but negotiate a work-trade agreement with that contractor. Everyone is always in need of something, find out what you can do for the web designer or logo designer and pay it back with work you can contribute and save your duckets! Start-up mode is when you have to put your church hat on—try to get as many things as you can without paying for it with actual currency. It is what is. No shame in my game and you shouldn't have any either. Remember the system in which you are working and if it's in the United States of America, then you take! Take what you need to move onto the next step.

There will, however, inevitably be things that you'll need to pay for and that's ok. As long as you make it a practice to "not pay" first. Explore all the ways you can obtain your start-up needs prior to shelling out what's in your precious war chests. You'll need to quickly be able to assess when you'll need to do a work-trade because let's be honest, you get what you pay for . . . and if you're like me and concerned with quality and brand image, then you don't want to waste time with a work-trade if the quality of what you're getting is going to be low or simply not representative of your vision. For example, I had one of my close friends put together the GardnerGlobal, Inc. logo for me for free, but we agreed that I would pay him for the initial web design. I knew the quality of his work and trusted that his quality would meet my standards. I saved some money on the logo design and the outcome was my first website, my first online presence. And it was legit.

When bootstrapping, be prepared to do and learn things you never thought you'd learn. Like a newbie, I didn't realize that websites need to be maintained and updated. There's nothing worse than visiting a company's website that looks like it was stuck in 2005. Not a good look for you at all. I realized that even in two years, things change rapidly—my own site was out of date. Not just due to technology and the real estate market, but because my entire business model was evolving. Team members, projects, and priorities were ever changing and we needed to make sure we were conveying our most updated status. After sitting idly by—and not being a web designer myself—I felt frustrated every day that my site was getting stale before my eyes.

Thank God for Wordpress! I had all my data transferred over to Wordpress, and in addition to being a law student, I was also on a self-created Wordpress website-building internship. I was in Wordpress every day when I wasn't studying. I didn't in any way master Wordpress, but I could navigate the tool enough to keep my site looking fresh for the times—I figured out how to add social media widgets. I learned that not every picture would be acceptable to upload, and learned about what size and pixels pictures had to be so they wouldn't be a big blurry blob on my site. In short, I spent the time to learn Wordpress to save costs on paying some third party to do so.

There were a few key mandatory business expenses for my start-up that needed to get paid. After starting a real estate company, I had visions of bringing on investors, buying investment properties, and away we would go. Except, I didn't have any money for any of that. What saved my ass for the first critical three years were paying these monthly, recurring bills: (1) Gsuite Google business to keep my emails active, $10–$20/month; (2) Email marketing with Constant Contact, $35–$40/month; and (3) Web hosting and domain name costs for the website, $10–$20/month. I was concerned, if any one of these items went unpaid, there was no business. I remember numerous times when I knew I wasn't going to be able to make that Google payment and my emails went dark for a few days. On several occasions, I couldn't keep up the website-hosting expense and my website went dark. I could let a lot of things go, but when you tell people you have a business and your business email doesn't work or they go your website only to find, "this URL doesn't exist," yo, talk about embarrassing! It crushes credibility. I quickly learned that anything else I wanted for the business would have to come second to the above expenses. The lesson for this young entrepreneur was "that other shit was unnecessary."

Time and efficiency is the name of this game. Since I was in law school, I didn't have much "business" so I focused on my online and digital presence—remember, my model is long-term and not dependent on a product I had to sell. In other words, I had to sell myself. And how I sold myself and my brand was by sending out a monthly newsletter or "e-blast." I didn't have any clients or business, but I leveraged news articles and I would find these real estate articles and include them in my newsletter. I would copy and paste the article in its entirety and I would cite the source, whether Reuter's, Wall Street Journal, or a local publication. I would always start with a brief introduction with thoughts on the market and where I thought things were headed. When I would include the link, I would drive people to my website with the article for web traffic to create a sense of validity. I did this every month on the same day each month. For $35–$40/month I was creating a brand, a message, and developing consistency among my audience. When it came to the newsletter, I would write every word, and design the layout. I didn't have a marketing team to do that for me. I would find time on the weekends—when I wasn't busy studying throughout the week—just to work on my newsletters. Often I would layout the next 2 to 3 months in advance so all I had to do was change a few words, add some photos, and press send.

If there is anything that I've done consistently with the business since day one, it's sending out monthly newsletters, that bill has always been paid. I remember sending out e-blasts monthly and being so nervous to press that send button. I believe at the time I had about 150 to 200 people on the list. I was always nervous because I was touching so many people with one message—I never knew how it would be received. Would people hate it? Did I misspell anything? This happened numerous times. Or worse, would anyone care? Obviously, I would get over that anxiety and press the send button anyway. Most of the time I would get positive feedback from people back home. Remember, I was in Grand Rapids, Michigan in a one-bedroom, semi-empty apartment. More often than not, folks back home would respond with words of encouragement and that helped tremendously. It gave me the confidence to continue building. There are folks on my email list going on ten years, and at my worst, when my confidence was defeated and loneliness set in, I could always count on a reassuring response from them to "keep going." I received other responses from folks who always exclaimed, "Keep up the good work" or "Seems like you're doing great," but little did they know the struggle behind those e-blasts.

Another obvious tip when looking to start-up a company is to work from home! Unless you're financed with investor funds to begin, spending money on office rent isn't an ideal place to put your money. Now, there are exceptions to this rule, but I'm not talking about the exceptions, I'm talking to the black and brown folks in the hood who go to sleep at night dreaming about their passion and wishing they could pursue their dream but can't because of their environment. I'm talking to that person who was raised by their grandparents because for whatever reason, their mom and dad couldn't raise them. The imperfect perfect child in the hood. You want to start your own business? Then use your laptop. You don't have a laptop? Then use the school library. No school library? Then use the computers at the public library. If you need to save your files, get a USB drive (you can find one laying around almost anywhere for free) and save your work and when you're done take it home. No money for a USB drive? Then create your folders in google Ed drive and start saving your files for free in the cloud.

We live in an era of advanced technology, which means you no longer have the excuses your parents or grandparents had to pursue their entrepreneurial dreams. And for the parents and grandparents that did pursue their dreams, I implore you to sit down with them and get some game! The ingenuity, cleverness and creativity for the past 2 generations to start up and maintain a business is something you can learn from. As you can see, as of right now, you can have a front-facing business that includes a website, email marketing, and branded company email all for under $100/month. And if you don't have $100/month to dedicate for your business, then you shouldn't be in business—you don't want it nearly enough.

Don't worry about getting an office or spending money on a co-working space. Just make sure you have some latte money, hit a local coffee shop, bring your lunch, and get to work. I made the mistake of getting an office space the first 2 years in business in Grand Rapids, MI. We leased with REGUS, which is like a co-working space but more professional. We paid $200–$300 monthly for one office that my partner and myself at the time shared. It was about 80 to100 square feet; it came with a desk and a phone. Phone service was extra. We left that alone and created a free Google voice number instead. Because we were embarking on this new business, we felt that having an office would give us credibility and therefore increase chances in getting new business so we took on the unnecessary expense of having a small office. Bad move! That was up to $3,600 a year we could have been saving to buy a property or beef up marketing. A large part of why we thought it was a good idea to lease office space was because when we finally renovated the duplex and found tenants, we started collecting that cash flow and felt we had breathing room. We were "feeling ourselves," so to speak. We were young, excited, and simply got ahead of ourselves. There was absolutely no need for an office space. Especially while in law school! What? Are you crazy?! We could have worked anywhere—the school, home, coffee shops, shit, anywhere that had wifi and we could have saved that dough. Not to mention, we couldn't just have any little old office, right? We hit the local Target and acted like we were on HGTV and went office shopping and bought lamps, decorative items like plants, pictures, and anything we thought would be great to decorate our office with at the time. So unnecessary.

We kept that office in Grand Rapids for almost two years. The last year of law school we decided that the expense was too much to bear. We went back to working at our apartments. More often than not, my partner and I were damn near joined at the hip. It was school and business everyday. We'd study together and then plot out our next business move together. We spent countless nights up together creating real estate investment portfolios, mapping out on his whiteboard who we needed to contact for our next move. We spent most of our time doing math, calculating the returns on investment for properties we planned to purchase. We eventually came to the conclusion that we needed a loan to be able to do what we wanted to do, which was to buy a property, fix it up, and rent it. Before we made the initial duplex purchase, we figured we would walk into a bank and ask for a loan. I mean, my mom always taught me, "If you don't ask, you don't get."

So, we walked into 5/3 bank and asked for a 30–40k loan to buy and renovate an existing property. I remember distinctly the banker at the time asked us two questions: Do we have any existing assets, and did we have jobs? I answered, Yes, I had a condo in Seattle, and yes, running this company is our jobs. She said the bank would not do any lines of credit because in 2009 the market was the shittiest it's ever been, and the bank wasn't touching anything real estate-related. Second, she said get a "real job" and suggested we both got a job at McDonald's. My partner and I looked at each other and started to laugh and both said "McDonald's?" "We're in law school, we're not getting a job flipping burgers." She said, "Well, I can't help you get a loan." Then she threw out the last option. She asked how much cash we had on hand—we had about 10k at the time. She then suggested we give the bank the 10k so that we could then use that as credit—they would lend OUR 10k back to us at seven or eight percent. We looked at each other and laughed, and then we walked out. We got back in the car and laughed all the way home. We couldn't believe she would even make a suggestion like that.

I was so confused and awakened to how if you're not paying attention and if you let your impatience get the best of you, you'd be giving the bank your money, not to make monthly interest on but so they can lend your own money back to you and make interest off of you. What the fuck, money's funny, mane! Needless to say we got creative, used our Obama financial aid moneys, called a couple family and friends and we scrounged up the funds to buy and renovate our first property. We walked into several banks and got the same response, no jobs no credit. Except, there was this one instance. An instance I'll never forget. We walked into a different bank and my partner and I thought, "Well at the very least, let's see if we can get a credit card. We walked in, I told my partner—who was white—that he should go in and ask for a credit card. Within 20 minutes and an application filled out, we walked out with a 3k credit card. That credit card was crucial as it helped us keep the small bills paid without stressing every month. Though I was 100% sure that if I walked in there and asked for a 3k credit card that I would not get it because I was Black. Also, I had about 5k in parking tickets from Seattle at the time, lmao. So, yea, there was that.

The credit card was useful. We used it to pay for the monthly necessities and we used it to cover some of the rehab work for the duplex (countless Home Depot runs). I think we maxed out the card one time while going through the build out of the duplex. It saved our ass and we paid it off. Credit cards are definitely a way for you to finance your business. I wouldn't lean on it initially (and you will) but it's a great stop gap in case you're running super thin. But make no mistake, your credit card should be your last resort. As you progress in your business you can use it as a point of leverage, but if you started out like me, you damn near used every penny your creditor would give you. Leveraging credit to build your business is indeed a strategy that most if not all start-ups utilize.

III. Survival tactics

The word started to get out that I was "in real estate."Though, not many people knew what that meant. Most thought I was a broker, which I was not. I was an investor and budding developer. I would get emails from folks asking for suggestions on the best neighborhoods to buy a home in Seattle. This was always funny to me because I wasn't in Seattle but for maybe a month or two out of the whole year while on break from law school. Another good thing was that people were starting to recognize me as an "industry expert." It wasn't the type of emails or phone calls I wanted initially, but it gave me an opportunity to display what I knew about the market back home. I'd engage in some light research reading local publications, but the source I'd always come back to was the City of Seattle and Sound Transit websites. I would inform folks back home of the city and county plans for light rail, community development plans, recent upzones, and what to expect in those certain neighborhoods. Although I was happy that folks were reaching out, I wasn't seeing any income from this advice. I would leverage my emails to people and pop them into my monthly e-blasts. Eventually, the calls and emails started to shift. I had a handful of people who were reaching out to me because they had no idea how to begin renting the home they bought in 2007–2008. They would call me and ask me what the process was and who they should use to lease their place as well as manage their home. Obviously I said I could do it.

Through my circle of friends back home in Seattle, I found out that a college friend of mine was in property management. I called him, one day "Yusef! What's good homie, I heard you're in property management?" He replied, "I am, they have me managing a few different types of properties, multifamilies, and HOAs" (home owner associations). I told him that I had a property management business opportunity and that I needed some help. I explained that I had a couple friends who are homeowners and they wanted to rent their homes and called me for assistance. I made a deal with Yusef: I told him I would handle all the administration side of things and all I needed from him was to set up showings for the units, meet the potential tenants, and execute the lease. And that's what we did. I would post the ads on Craigslist and Zillow, then forward any and all requests to Yusef, our "onsite property manager," for a showing. Yusef would arrange the showings and anyone really interested would fill out an application on site. He would then scan the application over to me, I would perform background checks online through a couple different rental sites, and if the application came out positive, I would notify Yusef to contact them for a lease signing.

Our deal to the homeowner was we would collect first month's rent in full for the service. I would then split that first month's rent with Yusef 50/50. This was crucial monies that I pooled together with the rental income from our duplex, unemployment, and a little bit of financial aid to stay afloat years two and three of law school. Yusef would collect the deposit, which we would hand over to the owner and he would deposit the first month's rent into the business account. I would either mail him a check for his half or cut him a check in person when I came home from break. Typically a lease-up for me at least covered my rent for my Grand Rapids, Michigan apartment. To be clear, I wasn't leasing Seattle homes every month. If we could slide in three to five lease-ups a year, we'd take it. In addition to that hustle keeping me alive, it would also increase my small business credibility. All of a sudden I had units to post on our website and include in our monthly e-blasts so it was a good look for us and I was able to gain some experience in leasing units. Simultaneously, I had a renter at the time leasing my condo on First Hill, the very first property I had ever purchased. I was able to use the lease documents from that property for all the subsequent leases I would do for others. Although I was 2,222.7 miles from Seattle, I was leasing homes and condos back in Seattle.

There are a lot of things people choose to do when in a bind, going to school and in need of cash in general. Some people pull up at the strip club for work (out of the question for me), other people become street pharmacists (didn't want to risk getting caught while in law school), and others find a job (nope, not for me). I decided to double down on the business that was less than a year old. I focused my hustle on real estate and the more I did that, the more I learned how hilarious this industry was, not because it was actually funny but because I was stumbling upon several ways to make money and all I could think about was how systemically the Black and Brown communities have been historically kept out of this industry. I haven't been in all industries, but while in real estate I've been able to tap into these various sources of income (sometimes, these fees would pertain all to just one property):

1. Lease-up fee
2. Monthly residential management fee
3. Monthly commercial management fee
4. Administrative fees
5. Resale certificates
6. Residential broker commission (percentage to the firm)
7. Collected rent
8. Commercial broker commission (percentage to the firm)
9. Real estate consultant fees
10. Developer fees (both fee-based for a client and fees for internally owned projects)
11. Project management fee
12. Fund Manager fee

The other income line items we haven't tapped into yet:

13. Asset management fee

As you can see, there are at least 13 different ways that income is derived in real estate. Some small, some large. What's been important is the business model I've pursued and the residual income that we have been able to accrue that allows the company to capture these different sources of income. You can see how things slowly shifted for us. At first I'd take on any and every thing that I could to make a buck. First it was volunteering my time and working for free; I graduated to taking on random ass projects that had nothing to do with real estate. Now that we've been in the real estate game so long, we don't need to leave the industry to make money. We are learning and continuing to learn how to maximize our revenue all within our realm of competence. In other words, as students of the game we realized that the more you spend time working in your field the less time you'll have for projects that have nothing to do with your industry and distract you from getting to your overall goal. I didn't find these out the first year in business—hell, I didn't know about half of the available fees we could obtain even in year five of our business! As we grew and as the pressures mounted whether economically or self-imposed, we needed to be creative on how to secure our longevity in this game and creativity meant building a vertically integrated company. And although we've had our moments of credit card use and side hustles, when people tell me it's not all about the money, I just look at them and internally have a laugh. Tell that to the folks who cut off my electricity and Washington State Employee's Credit Union (WSECU) who foreclosed on my condo in Seattle.

Speaking of WSECU, those fuckers. I obtained my first mortgage from them for my condo purchase in Seattle. I had managed to make my mortgage payments every month while in law school. I spoke a little bit about it in the previous chapters, but what I left out was how I was able to survive and weather the storm. I held on for as long as I could, and the bank essentially decided they didn't want to work with me. This happened precisely as my graduation neared.

But towards the end of law school, at the end of year three, finances were crazy tight; we were out of renters and therefore that additional income had dried up. I had a mortgage and had to get creative, and a mothafucka got creative. Before I go on, you're probably asking yourself, "Well if you needed money to stay afloat through school, why didn't you just take a loan out against your property in Seattle to pay for your living expenses?" Great idea! So glad you brought that up. I tried that. Tried year after year. You see what happens in a global recession is that property values decrease. Your property's value may fall to the point where the value of your home is less than what you initially paid for it. If this is the case, like mine, then the bank isn't lending you shit because as far as their concerned, you're "underwater" in your property and they will not lend you any money against your property because there's no value there.

So back to being a creative muthafucka—I figured out the coldest bank hustle. (If you've never had a bank hustle, then you've never been broke or poor). In anticipation of not having enough money to cover my mortgage, I learned that if I "sent myself" a cashier's check from my credit union's checking account via mail, it would automatically deduct (overdraw) from that checking account. I'd place an order online and it would arrive at my apartment in Grand Rapids and I would take that cashier's check and deposit it into my Bank of America checking account. (Note, I selected cashier's check because it's like cash, I knew it would clear.) Then, I would transfer that exact amount to the credit union's account to pay off my mortgage. So basically, I was having the credit union pay my mortgage—I would take the rent that I collected from my condo and apply it to the overdrawn balance. That took care of half of the overdrawn amount. I would utilize my financial aid, unemployment, lease up and any income I had to pay the other half. Now, it may have taken a month or so (sometimes sooner, sometimes later) to take care of the overdrawn amount in total but it wasn't so long to where the bank would lock down my account. At the top of every month, it was a process: wake up, go to class, eat lunch, do some "online banking" to ensure that that check was enroute, then go back to studying. I was able to do play this game with the credit union for some time.

As I neared graduation, I didn't want to take that gamble anymore. I knew I was only going to have a semester or two of financial aid and I didn't want to end up with an overdrawn account and a past-due mortgage. So I paid what I could but still fell behind on payments. At this point it was either pay for school or keep the condo, and I chose my education. I was balancing so much at the time. The new property, school, the business, my condo back home, not to mention the usual personal shit everyone in life goes through with relationships and family. I thought to myself that if I made a good faith effort to catch up on payments, the bank would work with me, especially since they are a credit union and they pride themselves on being a community bank. They would see that I was on the verge of being a recent law grad and finding gainful employment to catch up in on payments, which was only months away! I had scheduled to come home to Seattle for a visit, it may have been winter break. I contacted the WSECU's mortgage department ahead of time to schedule a meeting while I was home.

I remember it like it was yesterday. I arrived home and the next day borrowed my girlfriend's car to drive to Olympia, Washington to meet with them. I had written down the whole plan on how I was going to catch up on my payments. I was past the 90-day mark and the letters threatening foreclosure were plentiful. I rehearsed my presentation several times. I was nervous, but I was sure they would work with me. How can they not? It's not like I wasn't in law school and was staring at a dead-end future, right? I walked into the room with two white women. I explained to them that I was a law student on the verge of graduating. I stood up and wrote out my plan to catch up on payments within 3 months and they flat-out said no. I wrote out the numbers again, how much I would be able to make, and my plan to find a part-time gig when I came back home to Seattle. Still, I got a "no." They said there was nothing they could do. I remember feeling so defeated. I was the biggest loser in life. You couldn't tell me different. My first investment property was on the market because it damn near blew up. I come home to salvage my very first real estate purchase, and now I'm losing it to the bank.

All the hustles I put in motion to keep this condo for the past three years and this was the result? My family wasn't in a position to lend me the money. My girlfriend's mom at the time offered to help me by lending me the money, but I declined. My pride wouldn't let me. My ego was at its lowest point ever. Scratch that, there was no ego. I was froze with a constant grimace. The wound got deeper, wider and all of a sudden, the pain stopped. I remember feeling numb. The same coldness those two women were exuding in our meeting latched onto my heart and my mental state. I felt a piece of my soul go frigid. On the drive back to Seattle, all I could think about was how I wasn't cut out for real estate and how I needed to fold up the business and try something else. That or get a job at McDonald's? I saw my existential self, standing in a blood puddle of my own mistakes, watching my dreams pour down the drain of capitalism. Money has now become the purveyor of my thoughts, dictating my global paradigm; money had now become everything to me. I had been damaged by the same American Dream that gets all of our hopes up. An inflated dream; a dream that benefits only a select few. It used my hopes and dreams and profited off of it.

I was now indoctrinated into Amerika. Standing still in my own swamp of blood, paralysis takes over, euphorically. This was the very moment I looked Medusa in her eyes. And right in that moment, I suddenly wake up and hear the pilot announcing we have landed in Grand Rapids, Michigan.

Class at 9:00AM.

Recognizing Opportunity

"Opportunity looks
a lot like hard work;
there's no cheat code."

—MARK BAYSINGER

I. Eyes Wide Shut

'M WRITING THIS AS I'M FLYING OVER THE ALEUTIAN Trench, just beneath the Bering Sea, encroaching on the international date line. I've been hovering above the clouds for over six hours, and I have four more hours to go until I reach my final destination. I touch down in Narita, Tokyo, Japan for a layover then off to my final destination, Singapore. I was waffling with the decision to travel to Singapore for over 2 months; just one week and a half before the departure date, I decided to buy a one-way ticket.

I'm leaving Seattle precisely as I have client needs to meet, new clients to cultivate, and a new office that is still under construction. I need to finish building out the conference room, finish the bathroom, and complete the remainder of the carpet. I also have a team of 13 individuals, 7 of them real estate broker/agents that will inevitably have questions for me while I'm away for an undetermined amount of time. More than the questions, I'll have to do some work. There are plenty of tasks and knowledge stored in my brain that I have not yet transferred to the team. To be candid, I have not done the best job giving this information away to my team so I can step away and not have to work while I'm gone. Truth be told, even if I had somehow transferred all this knowledge and experience, there's no way I would be able to step away from my baby.

I decided to take up an opportunity that was controversial internally—I am headed to Singapore for a business trade mission as an Executive Member and Board Member of the Seattle Chamber of Commerce. The primary reason for my hesitation was financial. This trade mission costs five racks. How do I justify spending five racks when I have an office to finish building out, along with a bevy of other business expenses? In short, I could not justify it. I was going to stay in Seattle and continue pounding the pavement, generating business, and taking care of home base. Now, that's the conservative side of my brain talking. What does the entrepreneurial, risk-neutral, Carlos Slim side of my brain say?

This more daring voice exclaimed, "Nigga! How can you call chasing your destiny, your dream, living out the reason you were put on this earth, a risk? Manifest your destiny and take what's yours. This opportunity to travel to Singapore as a delegate of Washington State, meeting internationally known, high-profile and high-level politicians and business folks is not something you question. You have always invested in yourself and the business, why would you stop now?"

It's 2:30AM. I'm still at my office, and I'm staring at all the disheveled pieces of paper on my desk and the empty red cup that was filled with Pike's Pale Ale just a few minutes prior, sitting right next to the empty growler that I single-handedly took down. I turn my head to my keyboard; to the right is my mouse and a mouse pad with the company logo and slogan, "#letsbuildwealth." I begin typing a simple email to Harry

Cheema, who was organizing the Seattle Chamber trade mission: "Harry, I got my ticket to Singapore. Please make sure my name is spelled right on my lanyard. Send invoice." Harry replies the next morning: "Since I'm getting this email at 2AM, I hope you didn't buy that flight to Singapore drunk." Harry then confirms that he has put me on the roster.

I had walked home close to 3:30AM that day, as no buses were running in downtown Seattle. I put on my earphones, slipped my Margiela's back on, turned off all the lights, locked up the office, and started my trek home. Did I do the right thing? Am I focusing on the right priorities? What if? What if? What if?! (The crazy thing about "What if" questions is you can't answer them! So who gives a fuck about "What if?")

There were a few things that had pushed me to pull the trigger to buy my ticket and join the Washington State delegation to Singapore.

The homie: He's the only homie I know that can move like I can move when it comes to all-around traveling but most importantly, traveling internationally. He's the only homie who has an (Asia-Pacific Economic Corporation) APEC Business Travelers Card. Winston Victor Fitch—we travel to Vancouver, BC often for business and to escape the idiocracy, complacency, and normalcy that is the United States of AmeriKa. Months before the Singapore departure date, during one particular trip back to Seattle from Vancouver, Winston and I stopped by the local pot shop close to the border, bought some loud called Wonder Woman, and for 2 hrs had a discussion about the Singapore opportunity. We identified all the pros and cons of going on this trip, as well as every reason we could think of why we couldn't miss this trip. It was then, in that car ride down to Seattle, that we both made a commitment to ourselves that we could not miss this opportunity. Fast forward one week later, though, and I wasn't feeling so Wonder Woman'ish anymore. I came to terms with the reality that I needed to keep the funds I was going to spend on that trip and continue investing it into the business to take care of my financial priorities. I emailed Harry—who had told me I should really think about going weeks prior—and I told him that after considerable thought, I would decline to go this year.

The Seattle Chamber: I think Harry knew that I really wanted to attend this trade mission. I also think he wanted to get more brown folks on the trip. Whatever the reason, Harry and the Chamber were able to get me a reduced rate to make the trip feasible. I was looking at something a little less than the five racks price tag.. Wow! I think I could actually pull this off! And then I get hit with more office build-out expenses. I emailed Harry and thanked him for the reduced rate and the opportunity, but again I had to decline. I had settled with myself that Singapore was out of the picture, but damnit, I was going to bust my ass that following year to be ready for the next trade mission. I texted the homie Winston and reminded him of our Wonder Woman conversation, and then I let him know for sure that I was not going . . . that was until a little bit of Pike's Pale Ale and a reminder of my dream kicked in. If it wasn't for having a friend like Winston, who stays ready to explore the world and be on the international business tip, and Harry, who had bent over backwards to create this opportunity for me, I probably would have stayed in Seattle. It took a combination of things to happen before I realized that opportunity knocks in the most subtle of ways—if you're not tuned in to know when it's knocking your way, you'll miss out.

That same morning when I had finally walked home from my office at 4AM, I texted Winston a screenshot of my purchase: a one-way ticket to Singapore. Within a couple hrs, Winston texted back his own plane ticket. Like I said, not many can move like that. On some real shit, that was one of the most gangster moves I've ever seen. Who does that? Who can answer a text message with a plane ticket screenshot to Singapore? Winston, that's who. It would seem that I was not the only one that recognized the gravity of this opportunity.

When is something an opportunity and when is it a distraction? Is it all about "timing"? How will you know you're ready? You will drown in your own questioning, which is not a bad thing. You should question yourself often, and even more powerful than this self-reflection, you should have others question *you*. Open yourself up to constructive criticism. This will help you separate what is actually a worthwhile opportunity and what is simply a red herring. You gotta keep it real with yourself. If you can't do that, then you'll always mistake following your dream versus following someone else's. You're asking, "Yeah, but still, how will I know? How will I know what is a real opportunity and what isn't? For everyone, it's going to look different. Trust me, you'll know. If you have been working hard at your craft, perfecting it in every way, there will be no way in hell you're going to mistake identifying an opportunity. Fortune favors the prepared. It's going to feel so natural. If you've been in the trenches, on the grind, then chances are you've came across many opportunities and many duds. You'll be able to sniff out a true opportunity. Believe in yourself. On the other hand, not everything shiny and glowing is something you should spend your time chasing. When people request your time, whether it's a coffee meeting, phone call, or they flat out want to sell you something, vet them by asking these questions:

1. Will this immediately benefit my business?
2. Will this benefit my business in the long term? (what are the metrics/bottom line impacts?)
3. Is this in line with my mission and values?

Understand that you can get a yes to number one but if it's a "no" for number three, you'll want to reconsider if that opportunity/meeting is worth your time.

It's your time, remember? Have you taken it back? It's yours to waste. Timing is indeed everything. But it's your timing that matters, not anyone else's. Time is perception, and we all perceive it differently. *In fact, I'm coming to you from the future. I'm almost a whole day ahead as I sit on this plane from Japan to Singapore. You're asleep, tucked in extra comfy, lost in your dreams, and I'm over here lost in my thoughts waiting for the drink cart to come down the aisle.*

II. Trade Mission

Often the real opportunities cost. If you have spotted an opportunity but the costs are more than what you can want to spend, I want to encourage you to think about the opportunity at hand as an investment. I had to change my frame of mind and adjust the language I was using. Instead of "spending" money, I was "investing" into my business. In order to prove to myself that this was a business investment I had to lay out what the possible returns on investment would be (ROI). And I didn't just analyze monetary returns. I analyzed relationship returns, a much more complicated exercise. Business is relationships. It doesn't matter what industry. You may be able to slide by in the e-commerce sector but for the remainder of business industries, there is a human component that you need to master. I'm a master relationship builder so I know what returns I can bring to the company.

Singapore . . . where do I start? The experiences I'll share with you here in this book barely scratch the surface of what went down. I can write a whole other book just on those 10 days. I'm choosing to share these experiences specifically because they impacted me the most as it relates to business, namely the hustle. With that preface, let's start with a little bit of racism. That's always a solid way to introduce a story. *So 19 hours later, the kid lands in Singapore. I hop in a cab headed downtown to the Intercontinental Hotel.* A carry-on and a backpack is all I had for what would be a three-week excursion in South East Asia. I was half-sleep in the cab. Eyelids heavy, I rolled down the window to breathe in that warm, humid Singapore air. The cab driver strived to make small talk, asking where I'm from and what I do for work. I'm exhaling heavy as I retort. Head tilted back, slouched, the wind feels good—it's not cold, it's not hot, it's just wind—open and close, my eyes struggle to stay open. I lowered the window all the way down. Eyes fully closed, taking in the traffic breeze, I half-answered questions with my eyes closed. I opened my eyes slightly and saw lights, buildings in the far distance, a Ferris wheel, and suddenly we were crossing a bridge. Eyes opened wider, and realization began to set in. *I'm not in Seattle. I'm not home. Where am I at?* We pulled up to the hotel, where Mercedes sedans were parked out front. I stepped out of the cab and immediately smiled. *I'm in Singapore.* I paid the cabbie after he pulled my bags out of the trunk. I even had him take pictures of me walking in. The start of a magical trip. I thanked him for the pics and proceeded to walk into the air-conditioned, potpourri-filled lobby with the extravagant marble floor. I was wearing an all-black Nike track jacket with a subtle swoosh, grey jeans, and all-white slip-on tennis shoes. Although I felt the bags under my eyes, I smelled the comfort in the lobby. *I just want to crawl into this 5-star hotel bed and knock the fuck out.*

I approach the front desk for my first Singaporean transaction. The hotel staff person's name was Loh. I handed her my passport as instructed by the Chamber staff. She welcomes me. She begins to tell me about the hotel amenities and at this point all I'm hearing is "whomp whomp whomp." In my head, I'm like, lady, just trying to sleep. She begins preparing my room keys after which she asks for a credit card to hold the deposit. No big deal. Then she says the deposit is $3,000 Singaporean dollars. Record stops, eyes open, pupils dilate. "Excuse me," I said. I pull out my phone and open up my currency converter app: $2,196 USD is what that translated to. Now, I knew we were staying at a fancy dancy hotel. But is this the Ritz? Did I check into the Peninsula Hotel? I told the hotel desk clerk that that seemed a little excessive and that I was a delegate from Seattle, Washington, USA on a trade mission. She simply nodded and smiled. I pull out my wallet and realize that

I don't have any credit cards with me. They wouldn't accept my debit card to hold the amount. I had to call my brother—at 2AM Singapore time—and ask to use his credit card to hold the deposit. I finally get my room key and I head to my room, weary and tired. As I drifted to sleep, I wondered, "Damn, does everyone have to drop 3k to stay in this hotel?"

The next evening the Chamber had put together a meet-and-greet at the hotel bar. I went around and asked as many people as possible if they had to drop 3k for a deposit. Everyone said no; $600 was the standard deposit. So why the hell did I get charged three racks?! Unbeknownst to me, word got around to the CEO of Seattle Chamber. The next day, I received a letter under my hotel door from Loh, the same clerk who had checked me in. She apologized profusely about overcharging me. But the story doesn't end there! I saw her in the lobby the next night and she ran up to me to apologize in person. I wasn't having it. In a controlled, sarcastic, and oblivious tone, I simply told her that what's done is done. And at his point I could care less because I'm focused on business. Being Black, this kind of unequal treatment is one of those things that we have to deal with. THE BLACK TAX. They have that shit international too! Whether Loh was being racist or not, whether you're reading this and disagreeing with me and think I shouldn't always jump to race as being the problem or think I'm overthinking the situation, well, what I have to say to that is you are privileged as fuck to not have to think about your race as a reason why you get treated differently. When you grow up your entire life getting treated differently because of your skin color, it's kind of hard to not think your skin color has something to do with getting excessively charged for a hotel deposit, especially when it didn't happen to anyone else. This experience is called trauma. Anyway, that's how I kicked off GardnerGlobal, Inc. in Singapore.

I'm trying to find the words to describe this trade mission to Singapore. It was so overwhelming. Between the people we had the opportunity to meet and the information that was thrown at us, my mind had a daily meltdown. I had done a lot of international travel before, but nothing compared like this. This was on a whole other level of awareness, competitiveness, critical thinking, and preparedness. My global citizenship was tested—major props to the Chamber who organized a fantastic and highly organized trip. This was my first trade mission, which meant that this was going to be a "no distractions, no nonsense, let nothing get past me trip." A year prior I applied to get my APEC card (Asian Pacific-Economic Cooperation) in preparation for the opportunity at hand. While I didn't know I would be in Singapore, I knew 12 months prior to that GardnerGlobal, Inc. needed to travel like a diplomat. So when the trade mission presented itself, though I went back and forth, I ultimately knew I was more than prepared.

We started every day between 8AM and 8:30AM and ended each day at 5:30PM or 9:30PM and sometimes later—Rose all day! We had a jam-packed schedule that involved a mix of meetings at the headquarters of a few Seattle-based companies like Expedia and Amazon. We met high-level political figures and area C-Level executives. From the Secretary of Manpower to the Housing Authority, we were given a holistic view of how this small city-state is governed, operates, and has become the world hub for international business and tech innovation. The smell of opportunity, the hunger for greatness, and an unwavering persistence was how I woke up each morning. Sessions would sometimes be long, and sometimes the businesses, and people we met didn't relate directly to the GardnerGlobal, Inc.'s vision. Nonetheless, I went to every session on time, sat at attention, absorbed everything my brain could, and shook hands with past and present ambassadors. After all, I was not here to play games. My family did not sacrifice for me to go to my hotel room early because I was tired or to skip out on sessions because they didn't relate to my business. I thought about all the Black and Brown boys and girls growing up in the hoods of America and thought about all the ones who are hungry to leave their situation to better themselves and their families. In particular, I thought about slavery and what my ancestors would say if they saw me taking this opportunity for granted. Everything that our culture has been through and yet and still I'm able to have dinner with international CEOs and political cabinet members. No, no, no. I'm not here for games. I'm here for my ROI. I'm here to win. From rooftop discussions with one of Washington State's senior policy advisers to dinner with the Foreign Ministry of Affairs Ambassador at Large talking about her most complicated deal (which was, by the way, negotiating the lifting of sanctions from a Singaporean company who had done business with Iran). This trade mission positioned me among global leaders, powerful leaders who move in silence. I've always said that power moves in silence, and this entire experience solidified that belief.

It's another muggy and crazy humid Singapore day. Meetings for us have concluded. We had one last item on the agenda and that was happy hour at the U.S. Embassy in Singapore. One by one, all thirty-plus of us get on the bus and head out of downtown Singapore to the outskirts where the U.S. Embassy is located. Believe in yourself. These are words I say to myself everyday. And I was repeating these words to myself the whole busride over. I can't even remember if someone was sitting next to me on this trip. I didn't care. I was in the zone. The bus stops. Harry gets on the microphone and announces our arrival. We were given personal invites which we had to show upon crossing the line to enter the residence in addition to our passports. The security guard checks us in, we cross a white line and we are officially on US soil in Singapore. What an interesting feeling, I must say. Walking up the concrete drive-way we come upon a large roundabout with lush planters and high trees. To the left is the entrance into the estate. We are immediately greeted at the door by members of the U.S. Embassy & U.S. Commercial Services "Oh, you're Jaebadiah," Clint notes, the (insert title). We share a laugh and I say yes, I'm that guy with the passport snafu (more about this later). We walk into a large open foyer, where servers dressed in black walk around with trays of appetizers, wine, and champagne. I fixate my eyes straight ahead and notice the outdoor patio door is open. I walk towards the patio, the people to the left and right of my peripherals are a blur. I step outside and grab the rail with both hands, look to my left, and see palm trees and an oval swimming pool. God, how nice it would be to jump in that right now. I do a pano view to my right and I see open grass, backyard fenced in by palm trees flowers, and finely trimmed and curated shrubbery.

I quickly reach for a glass of champagne as the server walks by. I'm shocked as the time it took me to gaze off in the Embassy backyard, the patio is now full of people. Filled with my fellow Washington State delegates mixed in with local Singapore businessmen and women and sprinkled with a few ambassadors, past and present. I now find myself in the zone, GG zone (GardnerGlobal, Inc.). I slowly begin to raise the champagne flute to my mouth. I let the bubbles gently touch my lips as I take a baby sip. I smack my lips 4 times to accentuate the taste. And I'm drawn to my unlikely story that has arrived at this moment: South Gate, California. Los Angeles Unified School District. Public Education.

The evening unfolds smoothly. I'm asking the delegation leadership who's who in the room so I can get a lay of the land. I quickly begin to size up the room. While I'm plotting those who I want to target, Winston and I connect for a brief moment. If I can remember correctly words weren't shared. It was silent communication through facial expressions and eye contact. Within seconds of looking at each other we had a whole conversation with our eyes. Nigga! Where the hell are we? Yes, we're here. So let's get to work. And work we did. I introduced myself to the two ambassadors in the room and the US Charge D' Affairs. I had an empowering conversation with Stephanie Symptak-Ramnath. For meeting someone for the first time she had so many uplifting words for me—words that lift the confidence—words that create self-empowerment. I was shocked as I was expecting generic conversation. You know, the kinds that go like "how are you liking Singapore?" "Where are you staying?" You should try this restaurant . . .", etc. Pleasant conversation but nothing substantive. I had a moment with her that was total opposite. It was a genuine and real conversation and she pushed me to think about the work that I'm doing and how that's impacting others without my knowledge. She tested my vulnerabilities and insecurities all within 5 minutes. I was standing there smiling back at her like, who is this lady? She's over here pushing me like my mom pushes me—I took it all in. Every word. Sopped it up like a biscuit. We exchanged contact info and continued to make our way through the rooms.

One of the craziest experiences was meeting Mr. L—. I was in conversation with someone and a Chamber leader politely asked to steal me away. *She begins to tell me that a certain business man was there and was inquiring about who on the delegation was in real estate. Apparently that person was me. She briefs me a tad bit on who he was. No specifics other than he's a prominent businessman here in Singapore. She walks me over to him and introduces me. I take it from there and shake his hand and we begin to feel each other out. We quickly learn that we are both University of Washington Husky Alumni. He graduated a cool thirty-years before me from the business school. A Chinese-Singaporean and an American Black-Latino find common ground. I ran with it. I was straight up and asked him what he was looking for in regards to real estate because it's such a wide and deep industry. He mentions to me that he's interested in acquiring some additional real estate in Seattle. Of course I told him I could help him with that. I whip out my phone go to my camera roll and I begin to show him 4 different real estate opportunities that I had on deck.*

I was prepared for this moment. I had these deals on my remote drive but I knew that international data wouldn't run as fast as it would in the states. I didn't want to be the guy who was talking up these deals and spent the next 4 minutes waiting for my drive to load on my phone, then having to wait another 4 minutes for these large PDF files to load. So using a little bit of foresight I took a screenshot each of the deals so that when I do show someone in Singapore it came up immediately as a picture with no load time. What came out of that conversation was Mr. L—, the Chairman of a global conglomerate, invited me to dinner that night, post the embassy event. He asked what I was doing that night. I told him I was going back to the hotel. He told me he would have his driver pick us up, go to his office for a bit, then to dinner to further discuss the deals I had on deck. I accepted the invitation partly skeptical and partly excited. As the rest of the delegation was leaving the Embassy to head on the bus, they kindly reminded me that the bus was leaving and ushered me out of the Embassy residence. I let the delegation leaders know that I was going to stay and hang around with Mr. L— but that I would see them in the AM for the next day's session. *A few minutes later Mr. L—'s driver pulls up in an all black Mercedes S550, big body. Quick fact: There is little to no traffic in Singapore. Why you ask? That's because the government deters driving by placing heavy taxes on car ownership. But I would say the larger deterrence is car prices in Singapore. A Toyota Camry in Singapore costs over $100,000. Mr. L— had that S550 . . . with a Driver, that's all I'll say about that.*

In that car ride, Mr. L— taught me a lot about international business and I hadn't yet realized who I was in the car with! The car ride over was a feeling out process in the most forward of ways. Mr. L— used that time to grill your boy. Questions were a mix of business and person. At one time he apologized for his questions being so forward. I let him know that it was perfectly ok and I understood. But truth be told I didn't know if I was ok with it. I wasn't used to getting the twenty-one question deposition from someone I met 2 hours ago. I had to adapt. I had to be flexible. Roll with it. Tell what you're comfortable telling. Now it's a game. Share what's revealing without revealing. *I'm in Singapore in the back of a chauffeured car. Act like it! We pull up to his office which he then tells me is not just his office but his building. (Cough, cough.)*

Ok . . . the game done changed. The driver drops us off at the main entrance. We proceed to enter his building. It's close to 9PM. We take the elevator to his office and shows me the conference room where he asked me to wait. He disappears for about 20 minutes. I took this time to do some google research. I asked myself," Who the hell is Mr. L—? And what's this company? I begin to scroll through the articles: "Chairman," "purchases 5 buildings in Japan," "Partners with Apple," "Hong Kong stock exchange," "Thailand Stock exchange," on and on an on . . . *Ok, I think I now know who I'm dealing with. I immediately text Winston and drop my pin location. I said, "If you don't hear from me in an hour, here is my last known location. We both laugh via text.* I mean . . . I have watched too many Netflix shows to just completely let my guard down. (One thing I am not and that is a white girl in a horror film).

Mr. L— comes back and we head to a rooftop restaurant downtown. We walk in the bottom floor of a high-rise building and he's immediately greeted by the building manager. I overhear him tell Mr. L— that the Prime Minister of Peru is upstairs. I nod like, of course he is. We head to the very top of the high-rise and we step off the elevator into a very gaudy and ornate Chinese restaurant. We talked more in-depth about the deals I showed him and other deals around the area he was interested in. And needless to say, I had the best Chinese food I've ever had in my life.

Fast forward 5 months. Mr. L— visits Seattle and stops by the GardnerGlobal, Inc. office. We do dinner and talk shop a number of times during his stay in Seattle. I present an investment opportunity in a medical office building in Bellevue. He invested eight (8) times what it had cost me to attend the Singapore trade mission. Recognize opportunity. Seize it. Most importantly, be prepared for it.

III. Push it to the limit

How far will you go to experience the world? How far are you willing to go to experience happiness? What are you willing to risk? What are you willing to sacrifice? No shocker that the risk I took on this trip was unlike any other I've taken so far. A test of will, wit, perseverance, and ultimate control of my universe. To preface, make sure your passport is not going to expire with less than six months if you plan to go to Southeast Asia.

The devil is in the details. I decided to take my flight out of Vancouver, British Columbia to Singapore. When I arrived at the airport to get my boarding pass, the lady at the counter for Japan Airlines looked at my passport and informed me that it would expire in 2 months—in short, they couldn't let me fly out because Customs would turn me away in Singapore. You should have seen my eyes. In that one fleeting moment, my heart sunk. I started to get that hot feeling in the back of my neck. I looked around the airport and saw everyone moving on the go. The rain was coming down heavy. It was an overcast day. *I turn my focus back on the counter attendant. I pull out my APEC ABTC (Asia Pacific-Economic Cooperation) card and I proceed to inform her that I am on a business trip and I would appreciate it if she printed my boarding pass. She looks at my APEC card confused then repeats herself and tells me that she could not let me go. "I understand that my passport doesn't meet the expiration requirements but I paid for my ticket and I will be heading to Singapore. If you need to call your manager please do so because I'm not missing my flight." She gets on the phone and tells whoever is on the other line the situation. She begins to take pictures of my passport and ABTC card. She asked if I could give her ten minutes and she bolts off to another counter across from me. I immediately pull out my phone, email the Seattle Chamber and CC the Executive Director of the Trade Development Alliance. I alert them that I need urgent support to get into Singapore due to my passport expiration date. I ask if they could notify the U.S. Embassy in Singapore. By the time the woman at the counter returns, I have refreshed my email and show her a chain of emails started by the Seattle Chamber and ending with the U.S. Embassy in Singapore clearing me for entrance. I fist-pump, tilt my head back at the ceiling, and Rick Ross grunt. I tune my focus back at the woman at the counter and sign a piece of paper she is holding. It was a waiver from Japan Airlines limiting their liability on the cost of the plane ticket if I was not allowed to enter Singapore upon arrival. After I sign that bad boy, she prints off my ticket and off I go.*

I had boarded the plane without a doubt in my mind that I was going to get to Singapore. But 15 hours later (or so) after a layover in Japan, the doubt had begun to set in. When the plane landed I had a mix of feelings, mainly anxiety and excitement. I kept repeating to myself, "Believe in Yourself, you're getting into Singapore; there's no NOT getting into Singapore. You were built for this." I deboarded the plane and began to look for that diplomat/APEC sign. No checked bags, only carry-on—that's I how I roll (movers move). With my passport in hand, I rolled through the APEC line where only 5 people were ahead of me. The customs line next to me looked like a zoo. You would think at this point I'm running scenario after scenario in my head in case the customs officer denies me entry. Nah, I was as confident as Obama making his inaugural Presidential acceptance speech. There was no other scenario as far as I was concerned. Determined to enter the country, I walked up to the customs officer and handed over my passport with my APEC card inside. I stood there looking straight at him. He looked at the documents momentarily, briefly glanced at me and then the passport again. The next thing I heard was the sound of that passport stamp, "Bap Bap." He handed back my passport, I walked by him, then stopped to put my belongings in my pocket. I let out my deepest sigh ever. "BIY" is what I said to myself. Three days later, I met the folks who had made it possible for me to gain entry into Singapore at the US Singapore Embassy. I thanked them profusely. (Note: Does the power of relationships ring a bell here?) The chamber organizers told me that someone else who was supposed to attend the trip decided not to attend at the last minute because her passport had just expired. I can speak only for myself here: when it comes to business and family, I will go as far as I need to go to experience the world. I will risk getting turned around at the border of another country to ensure my vision lives on. I'll sacrifice money, time, and ego to make my vision and dream happen. Remind me again of what it is I'm risking? If my life and approach is a risk to you, then that's what it is for you. Since I was born, my reality has been filled with risks. The difference: I was able to convert my risks into experiences that yield learning lessons, growth, perspective, empathy, and much more. It's no longer risks for me, but choices with an a la carte or full entree of results. Push yourself until it hurts. And when you can't take it no more, whether that's studying, getting told NO, or family and personal pain. KEEP GOING! Slow the pace if you need to, but keep going. Don't stop pursuing your dream. After all, it's yours and it's going to come with a hefty price tag. And price is not always monetary; most of the time it is emotional and psychological labor and sacrifice. Regardless, if you're not willing to push yourself to the ultimate human limit to achieve what it is you know that's going to fill you with happiness and love, then step aside and let the other action-oriented dream chasers through. We got shit to do . . . like attend a Singapore trade mission and not let money or a passport snafu be an excuse to greatness. Find your risk tolerance, and be prepared at times to double it just like your start up budget. Don't size up your risks with others. Do you. Age, family status, and economic status (whether you come from money or not) makes every entrepreneur different. It's crucial you to find your breaking point, and find it early. That's your strategy to thrive long-term.

Hustle Inspired

"The company you keep has a large influence on the situations you bring to yourself."

—ERMIAS ASGHEDOM

I. Positive Mental Attitude (PMA)

SO WHAT IF YOUR CIRCLE OF INFLUENCE IS POOR? I greet every single day with an unwavering amount of fearlessness. I built my business on a single unchanging vision accompanied with an unabashed drive to see it through to its conclusion. I'm an inveterate when it comes to business, and although each and every day is different in its challenges and solutions, I've confronted shit I've never seen before more times than I can count. I'll spare the indolence for my future urn. There's something about coming from a place where every day you had to fight. So what if you're poor? Hope would skip my mentality like Santa Clause would skip your house on Christmas; I wouldn't even get coal. Yo! I'll tell you what, if Santa had dropped me coal I'd take it to the coldest place I could find and I would sell it, come back, and have my own Christmas.

Lack of hope does something to a person. That is the

ongoing, fight! Fighting not to lose your hope in the face of seemingly insurmountable societal pressures. So what if your friends are poor? These kinds of pressures force you to believe you are someone you are not, force you to believe you need things you don't, force you to hate things that don't exist, force you to love people you don't. It's all forced. And when I deciphered the world's coded language, I awoke to the knell of my forced future. A solemn future, shackled by student debt, mediocrity, timed vacations, and unhealthy relationships. In my mind there was only one way to avoid the story foretold by the 90280 crystal ball, and that was to hustle.

So, what if you're mentality is poor? The hopeless mentality took a shift when I had the opportunity to move to Seattle, Washington. Like tectonic plates, a slow grind would create rifts in what I thought was expected of me and what I could expect of myself. I went from eating tacos with security bars on the windows to eating pasta with a spoon and fork in high-rise buildings. I went from getting dropped off at a friend's one-bedroom family apartment to friends' mansion homes in gated communities. The economic culture shock was non stop and still to this day I continue to be amazed at what real money looks like. Some days I wish it was normalized for me. I wish I didn't react to money. Other days I wish I was a little bit taller, I wish I was a baller . . .

I would come up to Seattle once a year by my dad's doing. He lived here—newly married couple with a new baby, dog, and damn near a white picket fence. I came up one summer for Bumbershoot (when it was free) and we were having lunch in Westlake Center food court in 1996 or thereabouts. My dad, stepmom, and I sat together eating lunch and my stepmom asked me if I would want to move in with them . . . for good. Although this statement—by my stepmom, no less—caught me off-guard, I felt my answer was predestined, predetermined, and seamless. You'll have to ask them what my exact response was, but I knew in my heart of hearts, without knowing that I needed to move. This moment was a turning point and it helped give me the inertia to reach where I am today.

Those who have bequeathed Mom's, Dad's, Grandma's or Grandpa's privilege in the form of educational and financial affluence not only forget daily struggles, but have no life experience of the hurdles one has to overcome if they grew up poor. If you don't believe poverty can follow you into adulthood then take a look at the data in the PBS article, "How Poverty Can Follow Children Into Adulthood":

> Today, five years after America went through the worst economic crisis since the Great Depression, children are still more likely to live in poverty than adults. In fact, while the national poverty rate sits at 14 percent, for children, it's 18 percent. The problem is particularly acute for children of color. While white children experience poverty at a rate of 11 percent, around 27 percent of Hispanic children, 31 percent of black children, and 34 percent of Native American children in America today are growing up poor. (Source: Public Broadcasting Company)

To be a successful entrepreneur (and I'm open to interpreting what "successful" means) one must have the mental fortitude, yes, but more importantly one needs the confidence that comes with growing up in a stable and secure, healthy environment. Bottom line, when you have money, you're more confident, and you are less insecure—I don't need PBS or Columbia University to tell me that. It's not about the money. It's about the power that money brings. Otherwise, nobody cares.

They won't start to care until their perception of you shifts. Remember, you control the narrative. The circle, whether poor or wealthy, will use their gavel of life experiences to judge you. That's why all the black kids sit together at lunch. There's never a perfect balance. Everyone wants to find balance or have you pay them to find balance. But what the fuck is "balanced"? The only reason why shit works is because it's unbalanced and the hard truth is we all want to be on the heavier end of the seesaw. Sometimes you need more weight on the other side just to control shit, right?

And this brings me to my next question. Who's your weight? In other words, who's holding you down? Who's supporting your business, dreams, and ambitions? Who's there when shit is hitting the fan and you're on bended knee in tears because you have no idea what's happening around you? No idea what the foreseeable future looks like? Who? Who the fuck can you count on?

Who the fuck is going to be at your funeral? If you can't visualize their face, they gotta go. If they're not in the first pew, give them less time. Who are you praying with, building with, talking shit with? All of this will shape your business, what your client base looks like, and ultimately affect your bottom line. Remember, this is still business. ☺

Who's inspiring you? Who is that person constantly pushing you into challenging and uncomfortable spaces? Pushing because they love you and see your potential. Are you receptive to that person? Are you that person who always has excuses? Are you that person that talks about what you're going to do, and six months later gets mad at that person asking you about what "you" said you were going to do? Most people don't have that person. Especially in the 'hood, where everyone's fighting to survive their daily, worried about their next dollar. They ain't got time to be worried about you. But if you do have this person in your life, pull yourself out of airplane mode. Take the constructive criticism—take it personally and then make a mothafuckin' move. These people are precious and vital to your growth. You already get bombarded with so much negativity throughout your day, take that negativity and flip it on its head. Easier said than done, huh? Of course it is. But anything is achievable through practice. I can't do the splits but I'll tell you what—if my business was dependent on me learning how to do the splits, give me a few months and I'll be one flexible-ass CEO. Well, let's be real, at this point I'm paying someone to do the splits for me. But do you feel me, shorty? Inspiration comes in all forms. What inspires you? Find that feeling and soak it in. Make sure every day it reminds you of why you're doing what you're doing.

So what if you're your circle of influence's mentality is wealthy? Wealthy through education, whether street-educated or formal. I recommend having both in your circle. Though my law degree has opened up many doors, my street education has opened up twice as many. I remember a lot of what my Grandfather on my mother's side says but one thing that I can't shake is when he told me, "Our family came from the dirt." My grandfather's highest education is tenth grade formally, but he has a Ph.D. in the streets. The amount of street wealth that he has passed down to me and other family members is a blessing. And to think about everything they sacrificed—my Grandfather survived colon cancer, on top of housing almost every family member. My Grandma survived multiple sclerosis, had a front row seat to death, and still led with love. I was raised in a poor zip code. I was raised in a less-educated zip code. I was raised in a household where quitting wasn't an option. And I am supposed to be here. I'm supposed to be fearless. For me not to put my best foot forward on a daily is disrespectful to them and my ancestors who came before them. Their sacrifice will not go in vain.

Petrified. Hustle-inspired.

Acknowledgments

THERE ARE SEVERAL PEOPLE I WOULD LIKE TO thank and acknowledge but first I would like to acknowledge my ancestors who endured the unthinkable physical and mental anguish as slaves in America. I would also like to acknowledge my ancestors who lived in the pueblos of Chihuahua, Mexico and defended their land from the government at the cost of their lives.

Thank you to the initial GardnerGlobal, Inc. (GG) investors and believers. Huge thank you to the current GG and Onpoint team! Rachael, thank you for keeping my head on my shoulders.

To my editor Jordan, thank you for taking the time to sift through my Voice. To the secondary editor Morgan L. Powell, II. Thank you for having such a keen eye and providing my uplifting feedback. To E. Wanner . . . time reveals all, thank you.

Dr. Knaus, Dr. Marsh, Dr. Tuncap, Dr. Porter! You are all in mind while going through this process. Thank you for setting the example of what the power of writing can do intrinsically and externally.

Special shout out to Elena who witnessed this process and was supportive all throughout my crazy thoughts.

To the entire University of Washington MAP (Multicultural Alumni Partnership) Board Shumona, Mariama, Habtam and Kristin! Thank for being good sports while the impromptu photoshoot took place, lmao!

Huge thank you to my mentors who have all inspired me to be a greater version of myself. You have challenged my ambition but you've never curved it. Thank you Chip Ragen, George Petrie, Douglas Howe, Uncle Bruce, Dr. Knaus, Dr. Marsh, Dr. Tuncap, George Northcroft, & Dan Fulton.

Mr. L—, thank you for believing in me.

Thank you to my friends. Especially my inner circle, "togetherness is good" Douglas W., Mattew Kostecka, Ande "Greg" Paves, Lori "Shorty Cunningham.

My Pamilya!

Thank you to my partner in crime, Sumona Patel. We are still at it! Thank you Atuanya and LaVance for keeping me up at the most arduous times. Special thank you to LaVance for being Captain Zoom'ems and assisting with editing this entire book.

Thank you Ms. Ruby Jones for the leftover lamb chop some 19 years later! For your advice, guidance, and reminder to continue to shoot for the stars. Thank you for taking me in.

To my vision 2020 Bosses! Winston Victor Fitch and Anthony Taylor, thank you for the consistent push.

I can't forget about my cousin, Antonio. Always there to speak facts, make me think and have a great time after we handle business.

To my Compa Pedro Gomez, a.k.a Peter Gomes. Appreciate you Compa. In a short time we've been through a lot and have become close friends. Appreciate your ability to push the system from within in a productive way and be a vehicle of opportunity for our people. There's no other fresa who can do it like you. (insert strawberry emoji)

Thank you to (Kung Fu Tom) Tom Eykemans for the ideas and book design. Also for roof top Kung Fu and wrestling with the young champion in Brooklyn, NYC.

I have to shout out my guy Travis Senger for the direct and indirect inspiration to write again. Love you bro!

Ms. Priya Frank! Thank you for being such an inspiration and for giving me much needed guidance early on in this process.

To all my siblings Cymone, Xavier, Avery, Barry Jr., Seth, and Lil Jon much love. I hope I've been an example of what our family can achieve. Do more!

To my niece and nephew Jaiden and KayLonni, I love you. The future is yours.

Now this book wouldn't be complete without thanking my cousin-sister Lisa Queen Gardner and my sister Cymone. No one else on this earth will understand our pain. I love you both to no end.

Special thank you to my cousin Glenn. I love you bro! From shooting marbles in the back of grandma and grandpa's house . . .

Can't forget my mother Rosie Mosqueda. Regardless, I will always love your crazy-ass.

To my father. I couldn't do anything without the example of strength you've shown me.

Thank you to Tamara. The original source of #BIY. Thank you for taking me in when you didn't have too.

Abuelitos! Con mucho amor. Tienes mi corazón. Gracias for por todo.

Thank you to my entire family. Regardless of our differences, I love you and thank you.

I want to acknowledge all of those who have who have doubted me and all those who have actively put up barriers to prevent our growth. A sincere thank you.

Hi Five Levi! Miss you so much.

Aunty, the truest hustler in the Gardner Family. I took lessons when you weren't looking.

Lastly, to you, the most high, Sarah Queen Gardner. I'm just getting started and finishing what you started . . .

About the Author

J AEBADIAH S. GARDNER IS AN AFRICAN-AMERICAN-Mexican-American businessman, multi-family real estate developer, author, and is the Founder & CEO of GardnerGlobal, Inc., a privately held holding company, and Onpoint Real Estate. Jaebadiah was raised by his grandparents in South Gate, California and later moved to Seattle, Washington where he currently resides. Jaebadiah earned a bachelor's degree from the University of Washington and later earned a Juris Doctor (J.D.) degree from Western Michigan Law School. Prior to development, Jaebadiah worked for Turner Construction building commercial high-rises in downtown Seattle. Since then, he has built up a client base of private and non-profit clients in real estate development providing feasibility, pre-development and development services. Jaebadiah has built out a vertically integrated real estate company that includes property management and brokerage services. Jaebadiah has worked on private and publicly subsidized affordable housing workforce and market rate projects in Seattle bringing together city, community and design partners overcoming complex project hurdles. Jaebadiah is also a public speaker and has spoken at various real estate, community and higher education events. Additionally, he has held several part-time teaching positions teaching at the University of Washington, Seattle Colleges and the Year-Up program. He currently serves as a Board of Trustee for the Seattle Metropolitan Chamber of Commerce, President of the University of Washington MAP (Multicultural Alumni Partnership) Board and is a board member for the Pike Market Senior Center and Food Bank.